THE SUN OF JUSTICE

An Essay on the Social Teaching of the Catholic Church

by

HAROLD ROBBINS

Originally Published in 1938 by Heath Cranton Limited, London

ISBN-13: 978-0615981512
ISBN-10: 0615981518

For more information, contact:

Agnus Dei Publishing
1327 N Elm B
McPherson, KS 67460
+1 620-755-8832
info@agnusdeipublishing.com
www.agnusdeipublishing.com

O Dayspring, Splendour of the Eternal Light, and Sun of Justice, come and enlighten us, sitting in the darkness, and in the shadow of death.—*(Antiphon at Lauds, 21st December.)*

A King shall reign, and shall be wise; and shall execute Judgment and Justice in the earth.—*(Jeremias the Prophet.)*

Blessed are the meek: for they shall possess the land. Blessed are they that hunger and thirst after Justice: for they shall be filled.

The Hireling flieth, because he is a Hireling.—*(The Gospel of Our Lord Jesus Christ.)*

Justice by its name implies Equality.—*(Saint Thomas Aquinas.)*

DEDICATION

TO THE MARY AND MARTHA
OF MY LIFE

CONTENTS

FOREWORD

Justice, as well as Mercy, is an attribute to God Himself, and His Church is its Dispenser.

And if Justice, then Social Justice.

There is, I hope, nothing new in this book. It purports to be an Essay, based on the teachings of the Teachers of the Church. Such merits as it may have are theirs. Its faults are my own. That I have not erred negatively I have been sufficiently assured. But as my claim on the attention of Catholics, developed in the following chapters, is positive rather than negative, it is necessary for me, at some risk of being thought arrogant, to make a further point.

It may be that my discussions and deductions have failed to be as close to their great Exemplars as I have tried to make them. If so, the fallacies will be apparent and demonstrable. But if not—if I have really succeeded in confining myself to certain and probable deductions from the body of social doctrine—then any dissent must be expressed by answer, and not by mere repudiation.

For Social Justice is crucial to the future of the Faith. There are many ways to the Faith, but it is certain that the concept of Our Lord as the Sun of Justice is not only valid, but is the only way by which our disillusioned and despairing world will return to Him.

"He that made the ear, doth He not hear: and He that made the eye, doth He not consider?"

And if this were not so, we are bound by the law of our being to give out the Truth and Justice that are in our Treasury as soon as there is need. The day for misers disappeared when anti-Christ launched his greatest attack on the men of goodwill who, all over the world, are starving for Justice.

If Charity, the greatest of Christian virtues, is not emphasised in this book, it is not because its necessity to human welfare is not realised. It is because, in logic if not in time, there can be no Charity until Justice has been granted or achieved.

Good measure and pressed down, and shaken together, and running over, shall men give into your bosom. (Luke vi, 38.)

"If social justice be satisfied, the result will be an intense activity in economic life as a whole, pursued in tranquility and order. This activity will be a proof of the health of the social body, just as the health of the human body is recognised in the undisturbed regularity and perfect efficiency of the whole organism.

"Every other enterprise, however attractive and helpful, must yield before the vital need of protecting the very foundation of the Faith and of Christian civilisation. Let our parish priests, therefore, while providing of course for the normal needs of the Faithful, dedicate the better part of their endeavours and their zeal to winning back the labouring masses to Christ and to His Church."—(Pope Pius XI in *Divini Redemptoris.)*

AUTHOR'S NOTE

I wish it to be understood clearly that throughout this book there will be two classes of quotation:

(1) From Holy Scripture, Popes, Doctors of the Church and other authoritative sources.

(2) From Catholic and other writers, either on technical points, or because something has been said so well that it would be a pity to say it in other words.

The nature of each quotation will be a sufficient indication of the class into which it falls.

* * * *

To these judgments of the Pontiffs about Thomas there is added, as a crown, the testimony of Innocent VI. "His doctrine above all other doctrine, with the one exception of the Holy Scriptures, has such a propriety of words, such a method of explanation, such a truth of opinions, that no one who holds it will ever be found to have strayed from the truth, whereas anyone who has attacked it has always been suspected as to the truth."—(Pope Leo XIII in the Encyclical *Aeterni Patris*, on the restoration of Christian Philosophy.)

I: THE PURPOSE AND SCOPE OF THIS BOOK

Right is the object of Justice.—St. Thomas Aquinas.

I

Freedom is the primary and supreme reason for the existence of mankind. That He should be freely loved and served seems, so far as our thought can penetrate, to have been God's chief reason for calling us into being. At the cost of this freedom God could have established and maintained a world full of Order, but not of Justice, for free will is of the essence of human justice. As a modern writer has expressed it: "God so prized man's free service that He preferred a humanity sinful but free to a humanity of compulsory righteousness ... What should a man receive in exchange for the human dignity of a free soul?"—(E. I. Watkin, *A Philosophy of Form*.)

But by the strictest analogy with the main body of Catholic Doctrine, it is clear that God has provided in the breast of man, in immemorial tradition, and explicitly in His Church, the necessary elements for human justice and happiness, and therefore of a society which may best achieve them. The passion for Justice is not only one of the deepest instincts in man, it is by finding Justice that he recognises Truth. "The Catholic Church, that imperishable handiwork of our All-Merciful God, has for her immediate and natural purpose the saving of souls and securing our happiness in heaven. Yet in regard to things temporal she is the source of benefits as manifold and great as if the chief end of her existence were to ensure the prospering of our earthly life."—(Pope Leo XIII, *Immortale Dei*.)

This magnificent and Pontifical boast decides for ever that

the Church has her concepts and standards of social life.

It has been reinforced by Pope Pius XI in *Quadragesimo Anno*, in the following words:

"The deposit of truth entrusted to Us by God, and Our weighty office of propagating, interpreting and urging, in season and out of season, the entire moral law, demand that both social and moral questions be brought within Our supreme jurisdiction, in so far as they refer to moral issues."

They enable a brief summary like this to dispense with more lengthy metaphysical discussion. It is necessary only to add that although the Natural Law is the common property of mankind, the Church has systematised and made peculiarly her own all its elements. They are the source. The channels are the Popes, Doctors and Theologians who have stamped them indelibly upon the Catholic scheme of life.

"The law of nature is the same thing as the eternal law, implanted in rational creatures, and inclining them to their right action and end; and can be nothing else but the eternal reason of God."—(Leo XIII, *Libertas Præstantissimum*.)

This being the case, it is clear that injustice exists in the world because of the abuse of free will which we term the Fall. It would inconsistent with the universal mission of the Church that she should not have at command the expedients to rectify the social injustices which make up so large a part of human misery.

There have been times and places, usually limited, and always where simplicity was the keynote of social life, when justice was not invoked because it was present. A demand for justice becomes insistent and articulate precisely where it is lacking.

It is not without significance that the chief periods of Catholic social statement were the Thirteenth Century and our own age. The former set forth the Catholic Social Order with a force and authority never surpassed and still valid. It preluded and accompanied a magnificent attempt at achievement, ruined, as Mr. Belloc has said in a fine passage, "I, for my part, incline to believe that wills other than those of mortals were in combat for the Soul of Europe, and that … some accident of the struggle turned it against us for a time."—(*Europe and the Faith*).

The second and current resurgence was provoked by the impact of Capitalist Industrialism and its Communist development. It is this twist in the eternal warfare which has imposed upon our social doctrine an unprecedented strain and importance. The strain has been completely and triumphantly eased by the authoritative Papal statements of the past sixty years. The importance has been urged by them but not largely conceded in other quarters.

The Catholic remedies have been made available. Unfortunately they have not been made known. For it is of the essence of any major Catholic pronouncement that it is a reasoned case. Even in a purely doctrinal matter such as the Modernist Heresy, the Encyclical *Pascendi Gregis* presented a reasoned case. How much more in matters devolving chiefly from the Natural Law of man!

But on the whole, Social Justice has been conveyed to us grudgingly and piecemeal. The whole effect of the appeal to fundamental reason has been lost. It is the purpose of this book to make available, not only for students, but for Catholic working folk, *the vision of the structure*. For I hold it to be self-evident that a fully reasoned statement is within both the right and the understanding of ordinary folk.

To claim that the reasoned case has not been set hitherto before Catholics would be both absurd and uncharitable. But I think it is roughly true that such statements have aimed at the teachers rather than the taught. I have tried to exclude here all but this *vision of the structure*. The following words of M. Jacques Maritain, the greatest living philosopher, are pertinent:

"I have referred elsewhere to the terrifying lack of attention shown by the Catholic world to the warnings issued by Leo XIII with reference to social affairs. On the whole, and in spite of the effort of a few, who kept honour safe, the bankruptcy of this world in the last century in face of problems directly involving the dignity of human personality and Christian justice, is one of the most distressing phenomena of modern history."—(*Religion and Culture*, p. 31.)

The Catholic working man—to bring my purpose to a focus—has been told (too much and too often) that he cannot be a Socialist or a Communist, and that he is entitled to a living wage. Less often, and sometimes less intelligibly, he has been reminded that the Family is the Unit of the State. On the whole that is all he has been told. Certainly his information has not been on that plane of right reason which he is well able to achieve.

Mr. Belloc referred once (I think in a passage on fear) to "the succours of the mind." The Catholic body in England cannot compel, or even influence largely and immediately, the society in which it lives. By the strength of the case it should and could do so ultimately, but that is not the present point. Working folk are the infantry of the Church. They are suffering an attack of unprecedented violence and malice. Their bodies are beaten down to the mud of servile work and destitution, their souls to the mud of despair. It seems somewhat inadequate to attempt to raise and stiffen them by telling them not to be Communists, or by echoing the claim of their Trade Unions to a living wage. They need in full measure *the succours of the mind*. They need the vision, not of isolated brickwork, but of the City of God.

I hope that this book, written in humility despite a tendency to acerbity in statement, will soon be superseded by a better. Its class, if not its manner, is essential to our future.

II

This book is not an analysis of what the Church tolerates, and in tolerating guides. It seeks to be a statement of what the Church wants.

The distinction, which seems self-evident, is made surprisingly seldom. The Church has her negative standards, to fall below which is to fall into sin. These standards are necessarily minimum standards, for Moral Theology is conditioned by Charity. But she has also her positive standards, which are very different. I am informed by my clerical friends that the only name for these is *Ascetic Theology*. It seems strange to me that to want to do what the Church approves should be a striving after Asceticism, at least in its ordinary sense. Please God the desire is more general than that would imply. But we need not discuss this further. The point is that out outlook on society has been too much in terms of the confessional, and too little in terms of the City of God. A man could avoid the sin of being theologically drunk every night of his life, and give a very poor impression to his neighbours of the Virtue of Temperance. And millionaires are not excommunicated for being millionaires, but no one who is familiar with the blistering phrases of Popes Leo XIII and Pius XI can suppose that they are at all pleased that millionaires should exist. I see no reason why the laity should be pleased, either.

If, therefore, hours of employment, the living wage, and housing, are not discussed in this book, it is because they have no necessary relation to a discussion of the type of society which the Church wants. For nothing is more certain than that whatever such a society resembles, it will not resemble Industrial Capitalism.

III

There is a point which has sometimes been urged as a difficulty against the thesis presented here. It is that the Social Encyclicals do, in fact, discuss industrial problems at some length, in addition to stating the positive social teaching of the Church. But there is no difficulty or even inconsistency. The fact of such discussion is involved in the very nature of the documents in question.

Encyclicals are not essays, they are executive documents, in a sense closely analogous to an Act of Parliament. The Pope, in such a document, is bound by his position to assume that his directions will be obeyed, and obeyed at once. Such a document, therefore, necessarily takes account of the minimum of toleration in the system being criticised, and must make it possible for Catholics to live in that system pending its amelioration or supersession. It is clear that if the Industrial world had accepted fully, on the very morrow of *Rerum Novarum*, the doctrine that every man has a natural right to possess property as his own, many people would have been in danger of starving to death. For a revolution so radical needs a period of elapsed time, if only on grounds of public order.

It is depressing that it is precisely these points of tolerability and transition which have been emphasised almost exclusively by commentators and publicists. Depressing because the very terms of *Rerum Novarum* make it clear that the Pope envisaged something very like the ultimate supersession of Industrial Capitalism. If not, much of the document has no meaning. The Encyclical teems with such indications. Thus: "A small number of very rich men have been able to lay upon the teeming masses of the labouring poor a yoke, little better than that of slavery itself." Leo XIII was a distinguished classical scholar. None knew better than he that the essence of slavery is its denial of freedom and responsibility. He would also know that slaves, being valuable, were normally treated fairly well in material ways, and certainly better than the proletariat he was discussing. Therefore he cannot be alluding chiefly to low wages, but to the *essential* yoke of capitalism. Also: "Is it just that the fruit of a man's own sweat and labour should be possessed and enjoyed by someone else? ... the results of labour should belong to those who have bestowed their labour." ... "In no other way can a father effect [provision for his children] except by the ownership of lucrative property." And so on.

Happily, discussions on executive documents are not themselves of executive force, and there seems little reason to fear that the diffusion of property envisaged by Leo XIII will be dangerously swift. The danger and the swiftness are from quite a different quarter. It seems, therefore, that the mind of the Church will be followed, in this acute crisis of the very elements of social life, by transferring the emphasis from the tolerable to the desired, from the temporary expedient to the permanent solution. If you will, from Moral to Ascetic Theology.

For the greatest fight of our history is upon us. The gloves are off, no holds are barred. We should be traitors to our Faith if we refrained from setting forth, in the full measure of our capacity, the vision of Arcadia. Arcadia *has* existed. I mean actually and historically. But perhaps this is a suitable point for me to say that the Popes do not share that contempt for the past and that devotion to the dogma of Progress which have so obscured the realist discussion of human happiness. Thus Leo XIII: "When a society is perishing, the wholesome advice to give to those who would restore it is to recall it to the principles from which it sprang ... To fall away from its primal constitution implies disease, to go back to it, recovery."—(*Rerum Novarum.*)

And Pius XI:

"The highly developed social life, which once flourished in a variety of prosperous institutions organically linked with each other has been damaged and almost ruined, leaving thus virtually only individuals and the State … At one period there existed a social order which, though by no means perfect in every respect, corresponded nevertheless in a certain measure to right reason according to the needs and conditions of the times."— (*Quadragesimo Anno.*)

In the following pages I intend to bear on these passages no more heavily than is necessary to silence those who seem to hold that the existence of a principle or institution in the past is enough to bar it from the future.

It will be our fault, and not the fault of the Church, if Arcadia does not exist again. But we must not confine ourselves to echoing interested Bourgeois on Communism, or even disinterested Trade Unions on the living wage. We have more to offer, and this is an attempt to offer it.

II: REASONS AND FOUNDATIONS

Son, if thou desire wisdom, keep justice.—Ecclus. i, 33.

I

If we wish for an adequate reason why the Church should advance and maintain her standards on social life, it may be found conveniently in a principle which pervades Catholic teaching. It is best and most briefly stated by St. Thomas Aquinas (1. 2. 2 ad 1) *Grace presupposes nature.* That is, the life of Grace, which we need for our eternal happiness in Heaven, is not some floating spirit remote from the realities of earth, but is built upon, and presupposes, nature and the natural man. And since it is a direct deduction from this principle that the sound superstructure demands the sound base, the Nature on which Grace builds must itself be sound. This is not, indeed, to limit Grace. We have seen too often that sanctity can burgeon from a dung-hill, but it is also clear that the sound can proceed from the unsound only by heroic virtue, and nothing is more certain in Catholic theology than that the Church does not demand or expect heroic virtue from ordinary persons.

"St. Thomas teaches, that to lead a moral life, to develop in the life of the virtues, man needs a certain minimum of comfort and material security. Such a doctrine signifies that extreme poverty is socially, as Léon Bloy and Péguy so clearly perceived, a kind of Hell; it also signifies that social conditions which expose the majority of men to the close risk of committing sin, by requiring a kind of heroism from those who desire to fulfill the law of God, are conditions which it is a duty in strict justice unceasingly to denounce and to strive to *change*."-(Maritain, *Religion and Culture*, p. 28.)

Now the nature we are considering is human nature, and in its turn, human nature has for its necessary substructure the natural world. Since man was formed by God to His own image and likeness, he cannot be allowed to sink below a certain ample measure of dignity and sufficiency in the world in which he has been placed.

"It is proper to Justice, as compared with the other virtues, to direct man in his relations with others: because it denotes a kind of equality, as its name implies."—(St. Thomas II, II, 58, 1.) And "Justice exalteth a nation; but sin maketh nations miserable."—(Proverbs xiv, 34.)

From these principles arises the necessity for definite standards of Social Justice for mankind. Their terms are elaborated in the succeeding chapters, but here it is appropriate to discuss two points, the permanence of Catholic Social Teaching, and its relation to the fulness of the Catholic Faith.

II

The Catholic Social Teaching is timeless. It takes for its subject the nature of man, the one unchanging factor in social relations. Whether this nature is unchanging absolutely, or only relatively, need not be discussed here. It is certainly unchanged over the whole span of ascertainable time. So far as we can judge of Ancient Egypt and more ancient Mesopotamia, the nature of man, his motives, loves and hates, and in the widest sense his arts, were the same then as now. Therefore a major social principle enunciated not only by Our Lord, but by St. Augustine, St. Thomas or Leo XIII, is not liable to become old-fashioned or superseded. The point has been well taken by in O'Brien his *Mediæval Economic Teaching*. "One reason which suggests the View that the mediæval teaching is still perfectly applicable to economic life, is that it was designed to operate upon the only factor of economic activity that has not changed since the Middle

Ages—namely, the desires and conscience of man." (p. 229.)

The heresy of necessary progress finds no echo in the Church. A truth once stated is a truth for ever, and a new heresy is heretical for all that it was thought of only yesterday. In truth and justice, time is *not* of the essence of the contract.

But this works both ways. Most attempts to focus attention on the permanent elements in Catholic Social Teaching have been criticised too lightly in various quarters as appeals to the past. It need not be denied that in their anxiety to demonstrate the classic examples of applied Catholic teaching, some writers have forgotten to make it clear that the relation to the past is largely accidental. Nevertheless the evidence is valid irrespective of its age. There is, however, nothing static about Catholic thought. It is always possible that some new way of implementing a permanent principle may burst upon a delighted world. The whole difference between the approach of the modern world and the approach of Catholic thought lies in this. The modern world makes or adopts an innovation in social life, and *because* an innovation is *new*, forces it if necessary on mankind. Catholic Philosophy tests by the permanent principle. Does it further the dignity and integrity of man?

The world forces man into the mould or template of fashion. The Church uses man as the master-mould. If the novelty fits, well and good, if not it goes in all its shining newness to the scrap heap. This principle is the whole difference between the two philosophies. The world is constantly forcing man, in the name of Progress, into a rapidly changing succession of moulds of invention or fashion. The Church tests by the happiness and integrity of man, and by that alone.

Let it be agreed, therefore, that there are possibilities of human organisation yet untried, which may be in full accord with Catholic philosophy, but let it be remembered that there are examples from the past of full efficacy and validity to-day. An old truth is to be preferred to a new heresy, and a new truth is to be preferred to an old heresy. The old truth *has been* tested, the new is to be tested *before* acceptance and not *after*.

So much is clear, but so full is the modern world of the passion for novelty, and so much Catholic writing compromises with its fallacies, that the Catholic approaching this subject will be well advised to rid his mind of much cant. Not the new, but the true, not the tolerable, but the eternal standards, must be his touchstone.

Discussions on the modern developments form the second half of this book. The tests described above have been applied. Their age or newness is irrelevant. For it has been insufficiently grasped that cession in any guise to the dogma of necessary Progress is a denial of free will. It is the almost general acceptance of the principle that we are necessarily drifting into a better to-morrow which has brought us to the breakers of a lee shore. There is just time to haul off.

III

It is also necessary to indicate briefly the real relation of Social Justice to the full body of the Catholic Faith. We have seen that dignity and sufficiency are the right of a creature made to the image of God. Social Justice will put him on the road to Heaven; it will not get him there. It is of primary and essential importance because it is the basis of sound human life, but it does not ensure salvation.

The Church is well aware that her fight with the Prince of this darkness will go on until the end of the world. But she likes a straight fight. She has no use for the welter of confused motives, compulsion, atrophy and blindness which afflicts a people deprived of a sound social basis. She prefers a straight issue between the Seven Sacraments and the Seven Deadly Sins.

The real Cure of Souls begins when Social Justice has

finished its work. Rarely in history has that Divine Mission been so hampered in getting to grips. That this is no mere individual assessment is shown by many passages in the Social Encyclicals. One of the most poignant only need be quoted here. "Nevertheless, it be said with all truth that nowadays the conditions of social and economic life are such that vast multitudes of men can only with great difficulty pay attention to that one thing necessary, namely, their eternal salvation."—(Pius XI, *Quadragesimo Anno.*)

And let no one doubt that "God writes straight with crooked lines." We must hold to that for our sanity and hope, but in this matter, supremely, God has depended on man, aided by the full statement of the eternal principles, to work out his own salvation. We may remember for our comfort that as Leo XIII reminded us in *Rerum Novarum*:

"It is not rash to conjecture the future from the past. Age gives way to age, but the events of one century are wonderfully like those of another, for they are directed by the Providence of God, Who overrules the course of history in accordance with His purposes in creating the race of man."

Mr. Chesterton, in one of his most brilliant essays, pointed out that the writers of every age have their own notion of how society is developing, and of what the next age will be like. He added that the only common factor of these notions has been that they are nearly always falsified by the event. To-morrow is never like the dream or the nightmare of to-day. Our easy prophets depict a mechanised, a Totalitarian or a chess-planned world. Usually all three together. On the analogy of the past it will be none of them. God will arise, and His enemies be scattered. But let us not forget that the reasons for these falsifications of secular prophecy are the irresistible forces of numberless human wills, working usually in silence and the dark.

The Sun of Justice

It is our duty and privilege to supply the light which will kindle those wills to flame.

III: THE PERSON

Person signifies that which is most perfect in all Nature.
—St. Thomas i, 29-3.
Man is naturally a social being.—St. Thomas i, 96, 4.

It is the teaching of the Church that all human beings are *Persons*, but this word has been so degraded by careless use that its very meaning has been lost for most of mankind. A Person is *a complete individual substance, intellectual in nature and master of its actions.* Substance, again, is a degraded word. In Catholic philosophy, "Substance is a thing or nature whose property is to exist by itself, or in virtue of itself, and not in another thing."—(Maritain, *Introduction to Philosophy*, p. 224.)

In this sense it is contrasted with *accident.* "An accident is a nature or essence whose property is to exist in something else."—(*Ibid.*, p. 227.)

We see then, that a Person is not the same as an *Individual.* Individuation is material, and an animal or a stone is an individual, divided from other animals or stones only numerically, by being one of the species animal or stone.

A Person is a "complete individual rational or intelligent nature, distinct from, and incommunicable to, every other being, so that it acts *of its own right*, autonomously, independently of every other being except its Creator." Clearly, only a human being can be a Person on this earth.

It is by this philosophic distinction that we express the ultimate human truth that God created man to His own image and likeness.

"The word Person is reserved for substances which, choosing their end, are capable of themselves deciding on the means, and of introducing series of new events into the universe by their liberty; for substances which can say after their kind, *fiat*, and it is so. And what makes their dignity, what makes their personality, is just exactly the subsistence of the spiritual and immortal soul and its supreme independence in regard to all fleeting imagery and all the machinery of sensible phenomena."—(Maritain, *Three Reformers*, p. 20.)

It is clear that the Person, as Person, has no superior but God. He is not for the benefit of Institutions or States, but Institutions and States are for his benefit. They are to help him to his destiny, not he to help theirs. It is by the abominable veiling of this fact in the concept of mere *individuality* that most of our modern oppressions have arisen. Clearly, for instance, "the horror called eugenics," and the Totalitarian State, are incompatible with a community of *Persons*. They are only too compatible with a community of *individuals*.

The Catholic system begins and ends with the Person. He is personally created by God, to be personally happy With Him for ever. All Institutions, human or divine, have for their end to enable or assist human Persons to their final end.

From this decisive concept of personality arises directly the notion of *Integration*. The Word is becoming better known. It signifies that state in which all the powers of man are free to act as a unity for the due health and development of the Person in virtue, or with only such privation of goods as will be an incentive to overcome the human tendency to inertia.

All the powers; therefore that society is in harmony with Catholic teaching which permits or fosters the due balance of human powers. And all the *powers*; therefore especially those which depend for their due exercise on personal freedom and independence.

"The highest manifestation of life consists in this, that a being governs its own actions. A thing which is always subject to the direction of another is somewhat of a dead thing. Now a slave does not govern his own actions, but rather they are governed for him. Hence a man, in so far as he is a slave, is a veritable image of death."—(St. Thomas, Opus XVII, Cap 14.)

We shall see that this important statement has implications wider than purely political slavery.

The Person, considered absolutely, is self-subsistent and has no superior but God. Hence the unconscious orthodoxy of that most noble of human documents, the American Declaration of Independence.

"We hold these things to be self-evident: that all men are created equal; that they are endowed by their Creator with certain inalienable rights; that among these rights are life, Liberty and the pursuit of happiness."

But it is important to note that this equality is an essential and not a mathematical equality. A social hierarchy is not inconsistent with the doctrine, because it would be absurd, and destructive of the very purpose of Personality, to reduce the high diversity of human qualities to one dead level. The fundamental social principle, however, is that no such accidental inequality, in function or estate, may exist if it threatens or destroys the necessary basis for the exercise of Personality in others. All rights and liberties, as a modern writer has phrased it, "are subject to the equal rights of other men."—(Humphreys, *Liberty and Property*.)

The limits of tolerable inequality need not be discussed separately here, but it is clear, for instance, that they do not allow of a society which contains paupers and millionaires, for the former are deprived of the material basis for a true personal life, and the latter command resources so far in excess of conceivable human needs that they cannot fail to be a threat to the personality of others. It is deeply tragic, however, that by the failure to keep in mind the supremacy of Personality, so high and essentially Catholic a conception as that of modern democracy should have gone so disastrously astray. Lord Acton's quip that not the Devil, but St. Thomas Aquinas, was the first Whig, has an important application here. The present writer's own opinion, for what it is worth, is that democracy has failed, apart from the main abandonment of Personality, or perhaps because of it, by concentrating upon the relatively unimportant Person in politics, and forgetting the supremely important Person in society and economics, for these are anterior to politics. Or perhaps it was all part of the same plotting in Hell.

Government for the common good is, however, essential to social life, and

"he who has the of governing and directing free men, can be called a master. … But a man is the master of a free subject, by directing him either towards his proper welfare, or to the common good."—(St. Thomas Aquinas, 1. 96. 4.)

The majestic Catholic conception of the Common Good arises naturally from the concept of Personality. As Maritain says (*Freedom in the Modern World*, p. 49): "A Personality as such aspires naturally to the social life; it is a whole which seeks to be united to other wholes in spiritual exchanges of intellect and of will."

Such a society of Persons will avoid on the one hand the idolisation of Individuals as in Liberalism, leading to the very negation of its lofty principles, and on the other the subjection of Personality to the Totalitarian State in any of its forms.

Cardinal Bourne once referred to "that belief in the value of human personality, that insistence upon human rights, that sense of human brotherhood, and that enthusiasm for liberty, which are marked features of Catholic Social Doctrine." —(*The Nation's Crisis*.) It is not without interest that all these points, *except the first*, have long been familiar in political jargon. If only the first had been equally familiar and equally dear to us, we might be in much better case to-day.

A little reflection will make it clear that not only in social but in moral relations, the neglect of Personality is the source of our ills.

"All these conceptions misunderstand human nature and ultimately conduce to claiming for human nature the conditions of pure spirit; yet in the flesh itself and by the exasperation of a purely material power. It is a fictitious emancipation, the waste and dispersal of the human substance in the endless multiplication of needs and sadness; the control of procreation not by chastity, but by doing violence to natural finalities; the control of the race by the eugenic sterilisation of defectives; the control of the self by the abolition of family ties and unconcern for descendants; the control of life by liberty to commit suicide and euthanasia. It is remarkable that a certain conception of the control of nature by man is compensated in the balance sheet, with startling uniformity, by one same single consequence: the cessation of life."—(Maritain, *Religion and Culture*, p. 21.)

We need not be surprised that this process has been accompanied by a meretricious if temporary brilliance. The breaking down of a stable chemical compound frequently has such results in nature. The final result may be anything up to an explosion, and it may be long delayed; but the unstable is necessarily the impermanent. There are many signs that the limit of our impermanence is being reached.

Theologically, man is to rule himself by the four cardinal virtues. The special position of justice is stated by St. Augustine in the following passage:

"Prudence is knowledge of what we should seek and avoid, temperance is the curb on the lust for fleeting pleasures, fortitude is strength of mind in bearing with passing trials, justice is the love of God and our neighbour which pervades the other virtues, that is to say, is the common principle of the entire order between one man and another."—(Qq. 83.)

St. Thomas, in his concise Treatise *On the Governance of Princes*, has these two requisites for man, as an individual person, to lead the good life:

"For an individual man to lead a good life two things are required. The first and most important is to act in a virtuous manner (for virtue is that by which one lives well); the second, which is secondary and as it were instrumental, is a sufficiency of those bodily goods whose use is necessary for an act of virtue."

We have, then, the Person as the norm and end of our enquiry. But at the very moment of man's creation, God added, *it is not good for man to be alone.* St. Thomas states this, in the same work, with characteristic finality. He adds immediately a principle which the modem world has forgotten or despised, but which is essential to recovery on a Catholic basis, as will be seen.

"Now since men must live in a group, because they are not sufficient unto themselves to procure the necessities of life were they to remain solitary, it follows that a society will be the more perfect the more it is sufficient unto itself to procure the necessities of life."

Various institutions, of divine or human origin, exist to enable man to develop or maintain his personality. They are discussed in the succeeding chapters. The first and second alone are strictly of divine origin. (Discussion of the Church as a perfect society is not proper to the argument presented here. She is that guardian of reality who, pervading all, can be portrayed in no sectional study.) *The Family* dates from the foundations of the world. *Property* is its buttress. The first is essential to any society at any moment: the second is essential to its health, but may decline in its incidence without immediate social death. Finally, man has set up institutions to aid him, such as *Guilds*, which are the archetype of organic bodies intermediate between the Family and the State. And the *State* itself, that most powerful and refractory of the creations of man.

It is necessary here only to repeat that all of them are for man and not man for them. It is only instrumentally, and by way of unity in carrying out the divine plan, that man owes obedience to any of them. This obedience is owed in varying degrees, but arises always from the fact that Love, Justice, and Order are as necessary to curb as to develop the lord of creation. It is not good for man to be alone. His pride would else devour him. It is because the last two of these institutions are now commanded by men who are alone, who see themselves as making man to their image and likeness, that We are in the depths. The ultimate blasphemy is upon us.

Finally, we shall do well to note here that the first principle, of Grace being built on Nature without destroying or superseding it, runs through the whole range of social institutions. The Family carries on the work of the Person without absorbing or superseding it. The Guild and the State, in their turn, carry on the work of the smaller unit without in any way invalidating its position. The conduct and validity of any human institution may be tested infallibly by whether it fosters or absorbs the more intimate institution which precedes it. Any hostility or oppression of State to Guild, or of either to Family, implies its condemnation at the bar of Catholic teaching.

IV: THE FAMILY

Male and female He created them.—Gen. i, 27.

They shall be two in one flesh.—Gen. ii, 24.

There was a marriage at Cana in Galilee: and the Mother of Jesus was there.—John II, 1.

The Family is the primal human society, found everywhere and always that mankind is found. It is the archetype of social life, a true autonomous society. It is attacked and degraded only when human dignity is attacked and degraded. And it is the touchstone by which all human combinations are to be judged.

From the many statements on the primal dignity of the Family, we may select as being the most authoritative and convenient the classic passages of Leo XIII in *Rerum Novarum*.

"No human law can abolish the natural and original right of marriage, nor in any way limit the chief and original purpose of marriage, ordained by God's authority from the beginning. *Increase and multiply.* Hence we have the Family; the 'society' of a man's house—a society limited indeed in numbers, but no less a true society, anterior to every kind of State or Nation, invested with rights and duties of its own, totally independent of the civil community. ... Inasmuch as the domestic household is antecedent, as well in idea as in fact, to the gathering of men into a community, the Family must necessarily have rights and duties which are prior to those of the community, and founded more immediately in nature. ... The contention then, that the civil government should at its option intrude into and exercise intimate control over the Family and the household, is a great and pernicious error."

And Pius XI, in *Casti Connubii*, refers to marriage as "the principle and foundation of domestic society, and therefore of all human intercourse."

The decisive importance of the Family in society arises chiefly from two things ; the divine command to continue the race, and the human need of a close community in which love is paramount. These two are closely associated, but should be kept in the order given. Slight deviations in first principles are responsible for grave deviations in their applications. The propagation of children is the first purpose of marriage; conjugal and parental love the second. This is no other than the basic principle already used, that Grace presupposes Nature. The natural basis of marriage comes before its spiritual and emotional superstructure, however lofty that may be. To kick away the basis is to send the superstructure crashing. It is not necessary to our present purpose further to amplify this principle.

For mankind, the Family is a biological necessity. For whereas in animals the female needs little or no support or protection, and the offspring become independent very quickly (usually at the end of lactation), in man the female needs care and support during gestation and after parturition, and "the offspring require prolonged care and support, not confined to material needs.

"The human male and female are united, not only for generation, as with other animals, but also for the purpose of domestic life, in which each has his or her particular duty."——(St. Thomas 1. 92. 2.)

But St. Thomas amplifies this exquisitely in another place, in a rare burst of tenderness: "Before it has the use of its free-will, [the child] is enfolded in the care of its parents, which is like a spiritual womb."—(2.2. 10. 12.)

The case for the intimacy and devotion of family life could

not be more vividly stated. The unique fitness of the family for this primary function is due to the fact that, alone of human institutions, it is based upon love, the highest human motive. Other institutions have a wide variety of valid sanctions, ranging from ordinary economic motives, through a sense of public duty, even up to the love of our neighbour; but the love within a family is of a different and nobler sort, so special and exquisite that Catholic writers have not hesitated to see in it an image of the mutual love of the Persons of the Trinity. So august is this sanction, that only for the very gravest reasons may an external authority interfere in family affairs.

Since in no other human affairs do we expect and obtain the same degree of unselfish love and sacrifice as in the Family, any community which thwarts or hampers it is to the degree of such action committing suicide. But since the Family gives largely, it claims largely; and apart from the doctrinaire hatred of some who would gladly see the end of mankind, it is to this latter aspect that we must look for the explanation of the modern hostility.

We have seen that the Family, the primal and classic human society, exists for certain purposes. These are, briefly: the continuance of the race; the chief fulfilment of the human need for close companionship; the nurture and culture of the offspring. No more than any other human function can these be realised *in vacuo*. They are liable also to atrophy through disuse. They need for their normal effect a certain natural basis and environment. If Persons need for virtuous action a sufficiency of things, so do Families; and in ampler measure, since at any given moment most of their members may be incapable of securing such things for themselves.

In nothing more clearly than this have we shown our failure to grasp the implications of Catholic doctrine. We have talked all through modern times of the sacredness of the Family and the

Home, to the great embarrassment of the politicians. We have talked hardly at all, and certainly we have done nothing at all, about the necessary basis for their maintenance. We have striven to protect the effects, without bothering with the efficient causes.

Nothing can be clearer than that if the Family is the primal and supreme social unit; if it is to carry out so high, comprehensive and permanent a function; if it is to be *totally independent of the civil community*; then it must be furnished with tools and equipment for the purpose. And these tools and equipment must not be at the command of the state or of other men, but at the command of the head of the family.

Thus we come naturally and inevitably to the Catholic Doctrine of Diffused Property. The main discussion on this will be found in another chapter, but here it must be emphasised as necessary to the full operation of Family Life. It is clear that the Family should normally command its own means of subsistence.

"That right of Property, therefore, which has been proved to belong naturally to individual Persons, must in like wise belong to a man in his capacity of Head of the Family: nay, such person must possess this right so much the more clearly in proportion as his position multiplies his duties. For it is a most sacred law of nature that a father should provide food and all necessaries for those whom he has begotten. … Now in no other way can a father effect this except by the ownership of lucrative property."—(Leo XIII, *Rerum Novarum.*)

This is not a right to be maintained where, happily, it exists, and ignored where it does not exist. It is the duty of Catholics to work for its general existence. If "in no other way can a father provide for his Family in the Catholic sense, we destroy Families by tolerating a system where diffused property does not exist. That we are not allowed to tolerate the absence of such diffused property, even where the State has stepped in to prevent destitution, is shown in many authoritative statements. "Even where the State has felt obliged to intervene … Catholic Action may not urge the circumstance as an excuse for abandoning the field."—(Pius XI, *Divini Redemptoris*.)

And the Cardinal Archbishop of Westminster, even more recently, has the following pointed comments:

"Meanwhile, the unjust working of the industrial machine, which the practice of Christian charity would do much to remedy, becomes daily more evident. One vast item of our national expenditure is labelled Social Services and represents the cost—variously estimated as between four and five hundred million pounds—of what the community has to provide for the individual and the Family—pensions, education, meals, medical insurance, unemployment pay.

"And all this comes about because Justice is not at the root of industrial relations and because Charity does not rule their working. …

"No State can claim to be constructed rationally or morally, when one section of the community has to be heavily taxed to provide another, at the cost of its natural dignity and independence, with a sort of parasitic existence and a measure of bodily and mental welfare."—(Advent Pastoral, 1937.)

The Family is the Unit of the State. Why this should be so is clear from the nature of our main principle. If the State consisted of individual Persons, there would be every reason and excuse for holding that it superseded the Family. But no essential institution may be superseded; and particularly in this case, where the smaller Unit is of divine, and the larger of only human, origin.

The State exists to carry on those functions of which the Family, *from its nature*, is incapable, Distributive Justice, Social Order and Peace, Defence. It may not absorb any function which the Family, under normal conditions, is capable of fulfilling for itself. The Family is a union of Persons, the State is a union of Families. Hence, it is clear, the Family is and must remain the Unit, or Cell, of the State.

"From the beginning of the world, indeed, it was divinely ordained that things instituted by God and by Nature should be proved by us to be the more profitable and salutary the more they remain unchanged in their full integrity."— (Leo XIII, *Arcanum Divinæ*.)

It is of great significance that the attack of the Modern World on normal human life has concentrated on the ultimate human substances, the Person and the Family. Perhaps it has been even more active against the latter than the former. For if totalitarian despotism on the one hand, and industrialism on the other, can break down these two centres of social resistance into what Maritain has shrewdly called "a dust of individuals," there will be no social barrier against the reduction of mankind to a condition of slavery.

Father Vincent McNabb, than whom few men have deserved better of their fellows, has spent many years in the attempt to convince our world that the idea of the Home involves the idea of the Homestead.

"The Home is the Social Defence of Liberty, and the Homestead is the Economic Defence of the Home."—(*The Catholic Land Movement*, p. 14.) The point is crucial. Whatever is favourable to it must be supported and brought to pass. Whatever is hostile to it, however meretricious and modern, must be disavowed and in due time destroyed.

There have been many oppressions and evils in the past. To-day, almost for the first time since the old slave-state declined, We are faced with a general attack on the ultimate realities of life. The Feudal Lord wrought much evil. It does not appear that he ever thought of attacking the Family as an institution. The eighteenth-century gentleman arrogated to himself all property on earth. It was only at the very peak of his success that it occurred to him that his dispossessed victims were no longer Persons, but individuals. Perhaps it is time for us to analyse our own lofty phrases. Do we want Persons and Families or not? If we do, we must surround them with such buttresses as will reduce their enemies to impotence.

V: THE BUTTRESS OF FREEDOM

As a servant desireth the shadow—as the hired man tarryeth for the end of his work.—Job vii, 2.

The surplus of the rich is the necessity of the poor. To possess superfluity is to possess the goods of others.—St. Augustine: Comm. Psalm 147.

As with marriage and the family, property is an institution found wherever man is found. It is attacked and degraded only when a society is degraded and dying. And as with marriage and the family, the Church teaches that private property is a natural right of man.

Leo XIII has stated the doctrine in striking words: "Every man has by nature the right to possess property as his own. This is one of the chief points of distinction between man and the animal creation, for the brute has no power of self-direction, but is governed by two main instincts. ... But with man it is wholly different ... It is the mind, or reason, which is the predominant element in us who are human creatures. ... it must be within his right to possess things not merely for temporary and momentary use, but to have and to hold them in stable and permanent possession ... Man's needs do not die out, but recur; although satisfied to-day, they demand fresh supplies for to-morrow. Nature accordingly owes to man a storehouse that shall never fail, affording the daily supply for his daily wants. And this he finds solely in the inexhaustible fertility of the earth."—(*Rerum Novarum.*)

St. Thomas Aquinas, in discussing the lawfulness of property, is severely realist. He assigns three reasons why it is "necessary to human life."

1. Every man is more careful to procure what is for himself

        alone than that which is   common to many or to all.

2. Human affairs are conducted more orderly if each man is charged with taking care   of some particular thing himself.

3. A more peaceful state is ensured to man if each one is contented with his own.—(2. 2. 66. 2.)

It is to be noted in the statements of both Pope and Doctor that widely diffused property is essential and implied by both arguments. A natural right is the right of men. All men's wants recur, and are to be distinguished from those of the brutes, in the same way, by the ownership of property. In St. Thomas, it is clear that a peaceful state where each is contented with his own can only occur where each has his own to be contented with.

That this is the correct interpretation is shown by Pope Leo's emphatic dictum later in the Encyclical. "The law, therefore, should favour ownership, and its policy should be to induce as many as possible of the humbler class to become owners."

The point is well taken by one of the best known Catholic writers on economics.

"The individual security and the provision for one's family which man derives from private property are obviously benefits which it is desirable to extend to the great majority of the citizens. It is not enough that private ownership should be maintained as a social institution. The institution should be so managed and regulated that its benefits will be directly shared by the largest possible number."—(John A. Ryan, D.D. *The Christian Doctrine of Property*, p. 14.)

So emphatic and pressing is the need for this general diffusion of ownership, that both Leo XIII and Pius XI introduce the point into the wage question itself. It was said in the first chapter that the temporary tolerations and expedients of the Church would not be discussed in this book, but the evidence that they are temporary is so clear from the Papal treatment as to justify quotation here.

"It is surely undeniable that when a man engages in remunerative labour, the impelling reason and motive of his work is to obtain property, and thereafter to hold it as his very own ... If a workman's wages be sufficient to enable him to maintain himself, his wife and his children in reasonable comfort, he will not find it difficult, if he be a sensible man, to study economy; and he will not fail, by cutting down expenses, to put by some little savings and thus secure a small income ... If working folk can be encouraged to look forward to obtaining a share in the land ... the gulf between vast wealth and sheer poverty will be bridged over."—(*Rerum Novarum.*)

"This is the aim which Our Predecessor urged as the necessary object of Our efforts: the uplifting of the proletariat ... The number of the dispossessed labouring masses, whose groans mount to Heaven from these lands, increased beyond all measure. Moreover, there is the immense army of hired rural labourers, whose condition is depressed in the extreme, and who have no hope of ever obtaining a share in the land. These too unless efficacious remedies be applied will remain perpetually SUNK [capitals mine] in their proletarian condition. ... Every effort must be made that ... an ample sufficiency be supplied to the working man. The purpose is not that these become slack at their work, for man is born to labour as the birds to fly, but that by thrift they may increase their possessions ... This programme cannot, however, be realised unless the propertyless wage-earner be placed in such circumstances that by skill and thrift he can acquire a certain moderate ownership ... But how can he ever save money except from his wages?"—(*Quadragesimo Anno.*)

It is clear, therefore, that in the mind of the Church, wages under Industrialism or any other system should be not only sufficient for the reasonable comfort of the family, but should permit of saving to acquire property.

It is not necessary to emphasise that in no country do wages approach this level. The system, therefore, as it exists, is without even the *toleration* of the Church.

The alternative means, by which the natural right to property may generally be achieved, have not yet been stated, and Catholics are free to implement the principle in any way consistent with good morals. Perhaps there is a hint in the latest Encyclical of the present Pope.

"It must likewise be the special care of the State to create those material conditions of life without which an orderly society cannot exist. The State must take every measure necessary to supply employment, particularly for the heads of families and for the young. To achieve this end demanded by the pressing needs of the common welfare, the wealthy classes must be induced to assume those burdens without which human society cannot be saved nor they themselves remain secure. *However, measures taken by the State with this end in view ought to be of such a nature that they will really affect those who actually possess more than their share of capital resources, and who continue to accumulate them to the grievous detriment of others.*"—(*Divini redemptoris.*) The Italics are mine.

Moreover, it is part of Catholic teaching that extreme need confers a right of participation in the goods of others.

"All things are common property in a case of extreme necessity. Hence one who is in such dire straits may take another's goods in order to succour himself, if he can find no one who is willing to give him something."—(St. Thomas 2. 2. 32. 7.)

Finally, there is the noble statement of our own Saint Thomas More:

"Thou wilt what if I cannot labour, or have more small children to find than my labour of three days will suffice to feed for one day, shall I not then care and take thought how they shall live to-morrow? Or tell what other shift I shall find. First shall I tell thee what shift thou shalt make in such case; and after shall I shew thee that, if all shift fail thee, yet if thou be a faithful man thou shalt take no thought? I say if thou lack, thou shalt labour to thy power by just and true business to get that thee and thine behoveth. If thy labour suffice not, thou shalt shew thy state, that thou hast little money and much charge, to some such men as have much money and little charge, *and they be bounden of duty to supply of theirs that thee lacketh of thine.*"—(*The Four Last Things.*) The italics, I regret to say, are mine. It did not occur to the saintly and distinguished author that they would be necessary.

The benefits of diffused property are striking and decisive. Philosophically, we may assess them in three groups.

1. They are a buttress to freedom, because they make men independent of the domination of other human wills. This is as striking spiritually as socially and economically, for the "fear of the sack," or extreme poverty, is a deterrent to the good use of reason, and frequently to good morals.

2. They promote the common good, for where property is equitably divided, great wealth and great poverty, both corrupters of good morals and order, are unlikely and rare.

3. The best possible use is made of productive powers. It is remarkable that this is not accepted more generally, for men who possess property cannot fail to recognise its magic in promoting harder and more intelligent work, even when they deny or ignore its equal possibilities for others.

Moreover, this is one of the cases where we have a direct and emphatic lead from Our Lord Himself. In one of His most touching parables, He says, so simply that it is clear He the fact as self-evident :

"The Hireling flieth, because he is a Hireling."—(John x, 13.)

Those eight words are themselves a complete condemnation of a system in which the Hireling is normal. Our Lord does not condemn the Hireling. He flies, not because he is a coward or a villain, but because he is a Hireling, and clearly no state in which the bulk of the people are of this category can attain either a real organic order, or a true civilisation. The point need not be elaborated.

In none of their aspects have the stipulations of the Papal Encyclicals been accepted and worked for by Catholics generally. The failure or refusal to do so is disgraceful to us. Pius XI says grimly, in *Quadragesimo Anno*, "This state of things was quite satisfactory to the wealthy." It appears to have been equally satisfactory in other and more surprising quarters. Catholic Employers, in England at any rate, have made no noticeable attempt to implement even the temporary expedients. As regards the permanent remedies, nothing has been done at all. A well-known and influential Catholic layman recently had the hardihood to say: "I confess I see no real remedy in encouraging an artisan to hold property." This was six years after *Quadragesimo Anno*, forty-six years after *Rerum Novarum*, about seven hundred after Saint Thomas, and nineteen hundred after Our Lord said "The Hireling flieth, because he is a Hireling."

Other words of Our Lord are very much overworked. "The poor you have always with you," means something quite different from its use by the wealthy, but it is seen very frequently indeed. Perhaps if we overwork the definite reference to the Hireling our rich will be persuaded to do something about him.

It is important to note that Capitalism is not capable of direct censure, because it is only indirectly, by casual monopoly so to speak, that it denies property to the bulk of mankind. As Mr. Belloc reminds us in his *Catholic Church and the Principle of Private Property*, Capitalism is a disease of Property.

"Unfortunately, Industrial Capitalism was not susceptible of direct ecclesiastical censure, though all its unwritten first principles had been denounced from the very origins of the Catholic church, first by its Divine Founder, lastly in the Encyclicals of Leo XIII and Pius X, and now in *Quadragesimo Anno.*"—(p. 15.)

He adds, and the words, to anyone who has studied the thing, are not immoderate :

"The avarice, the contempt for mercy and justice, the bestial lack of reason and almost equally bestial lack of art in this evil thing, sufficiently show from what seed it sprang. The reproach that individual Catholics rarely flourish in its atmosphere should be not be a reproach to us but a glory."—(*Ibid.*, p. 16.)

It is pertinent to add a word of warning, which may be given in the words of the same distinguished writer.

"Finally, this function of property, like all other human attributes, is distorted when it is defined in isolation. It must be taken in with the mass of all other human functions, and is subject, as is every one of them, to the general modification imposed by the generalities of human existence."—(*Ibid.*, p. 6.)

I propose, for this and other reasons, to defer to later chapters on the Guild, Industrialism and Commerce, other aspects of this function of property.

This chapter may end fitly with a brief analysis of a modern fallacy.

The modern world began with a position where economic power was fairly widely diffused among the people, but political power was highly concentrated in nominally absolute monarchies run actually by the very rich. It is deplorable, but not surprising, that the struggle for political freedom absorbed the general attention. The purely economic onslaught of the very rich was delivered with little conscious opposition until it was too late. The diabolical selfishness of the squires who drove their surplus labourers into the towns by a series of frauds, beginning with enclosures and ending with the razing of cottages, coincided with the introduction of machinery and the factory system. It is a melancholy compensation that their act sealed their own doom as a class. But the dominance of the purely political approach remained. Nevertheless it is true that there is no real political power without economic power as a basis.

In the peculiar conditions of the present, where both political and economic power are lacking to the bulk of the citizens, it will be necessary to react on both fronts simultaneously. But it is true that in the long run, political power can only exist where economic power is present. It is necessary only to prevent the rich from concentrating again on one of them behind the smoke screen of the other.

VI: THE GUILD AND THE JUST PRICE

A brother that is helped by his brother, is like a strong city.
—Proverbs xviii, 19.

To desire to buy a thing too cheaply, and to sell a thing too dearly, is truly a sin.—St. Augustine 13, De Trin. 7.

I

The deeply rooted social instincts of mankind have urged him at all times to join with his fellows in groups larger than those permitted by the family, for devotional, charitable, convivial or economic purposes. They are older and more widely spread than the Catholic Faith. They were known in all the ancient civilisations, and exist to-day, often in striking forms, in China, India and elsewhere. But it is in the Mediæval Catholic culture that we find their finest and most general expression.

The impulse to associate with one's fellows there took many forms, often with lofty and touching ideals and practice. To adorn the fabric of a church, to build bridges, to care for the sick and needy, are some of their objects. The present work need only refer to them as striking spontaneous evidence of the need for social life in man, fittingly realised. The Craft Guild, with which were often associated by way of human integrity the other purposes referred to, is the archetype and crown of the human association. They added to any other object, as a principal object, the sanctification of the lives of the members by dignity and integrity of work. The Guild also is the natural right of man. Leo XIII states explicitly: "To enter into a society of this kind is the natural right of man, and the state is bound to protect natural rights, not to destroy them; and if it forbid citizens to form associations, it contradicts the very principle of its own existence, for both they and it exist in virtue of the like principle, namely, the natural tendency of man to dwell in society."—(*Rerum Novarum.*)

He supports the claim by quoting a passage from Holy Writ. "It is better that two should be together than one; for they have the advantage of their society. If one fall he shall be supported by the other. Woe to him that is alone, for when he falleth he hath none to lift him up."—(Ecclesiastes iv, 9-10.)

It is important to note at once this characteristic basis of the Guild. It does not supplant or absorb, it cherishes and reinforces. We are beginning to see the universal and pervading spirit of the Catholic order. The larger and wider association never supplants the smaller and more intimate one. As Pius XI says:

"It is an injustice, a grave evil and a disturbance of right order, for a larger and higher organisation to arrogate to itself functions which can be performed efficiently by smaller and lower bodies. This is a fundamental principle of social philosophy, unshaken and unchangeable."—(*Quadragesimo Anno.*)

Applying the same principle to marriage, he says in *Casti Connubii* that her position in the family "does not deny or take away the liberty which fully belongs to the woman both in view of her dignity as a human person … and of her most noble office as wife and mother and companion."

Thus the Person is helped, but not absorbed or supplanted, by the Family, the Family by the Institution of Property: both by the Guild, and all by the State. The functions of each successive institution are limited to what cannot be carried out fittingly by its predecessors.

We should be clear on this at the outset, for it is when we come to consider the Guild that misconception is most rife. The Guild, in its classic Catholic form, never absorbed or changed the basis of personal property and livelihood. It was not a profit-sharing factory, but an association of free integral producers for their mutual advantage and succour.

That this is so is clear from all the histories. O'Brien, for example, has this passage:

"The whole fabric of Mediæval economics was based on the foundation of private property, and the elaborate and logical system of regulations to ensure justice in economic life would have had no purpose or no use if the subject-matter of that justice were abolished."—(*Op. cit.*, p. 40.)

We may note, further, an interesting point which brings out this underlying basis.

The late Arthur Penty, in his *Guildsman's Interpretation of History*, discusses the causes of the Guild failure in ancient Rome, and notes that in addition to that of too exclusive an attention to material things it was due to the operation of the Roman Law. "It was, in fact, a system of law designed primarily for the purpose of enabling rich men to live among poor, as emphatically as the Canon Law was designed to enable good men to live among bad." (p. 63.) He assigns to the revival of Roman Law in Europe the chief part in the destruction of the Guilds. The statement is striking and probably true. If so, we have here a unique testimony to the validity and purpose of Catholic social teaching.

The Guild, then, was a spontaneous growth of associations to protect and succour families in their social and economic relations. To enable the products of domestic crafts to be sold at a just price, to prevent exploitation of the poor in work by the apprentice system leading inevitably to Mastership, to maintain high standards of craftsmanship, to provide for the needy, the aged and the unfortunate, to worship in common. These were the real, and not merely the ideal, fruits of the Guild System.

Penty considers that its weakness was that it was confined to the towns. Had it been extended to rural crafts and to agriculture, he says, it might have survived. This may well be true. There was no reason against Guilds of Agriculture except the incubus of the feudal system. (Apart from other defects, the Modern Marketing Boards will never develop into true Guilds because they contravene the first canon of art. They do not accept the properties and limits of the material they work in. Agriculture is one, and an Agricultural Guild must be one. To isolate products, as milk or meat, is in the special circumstances an absurdity.)

However that may be, it is clear that the Guild principle of free spontaneous association can take us far on the road of self-government, relieving the State of much detailed administration for which it is unfitted.

"These groups, in a true sense autonomous, are considered by many to be, if not essential to civil society, at least its natural and spontaneous development. …

"Those who are engaged in the same trade or profession will form free associations among themselves for purposes connected with their occupations."—(Pius XI, *Quadragesimo Anno.*)

II

A great part of *Rerum Novarum* is taken up with the case for the right of association by workmen, then being denied or very grudgingly admitted. Leo XIII had Trade Unions chiefly in mind, and mentions Guilds only to regret their destruction.

In *Quadragesimo Anno*, the position allocated by Pope Pius XI to "Guilds" is highly significant. After the general historical preamble of section I, he gives priority in section II to paragraphs entitled respectively The Right to Property, Its Individual and Social Character, The Obligations of Ownership, and several other subsidiary points, culminating in Principle of Just Distribution and The Uplifting of the Proletariat. Then follow the paragraphs already discussed, in the course of which he indicates the property motive underlying the just wage. On this avowed basis, he then turns to the consideration of "Vocational Groups," as being a *social* development from what he has said. The order, as well as the matter, is essential to correct interpretation. Some six pages are devoted to "Vocational Groups." The Latin original for this phrase is *Ordines*. The reason for the precise phrase selected by the translator has not been explained up to the present. From the context, it does not appear that the Pope intended to introduce any innovation, but to recommend various organic groups of the citizens, especially "Guilds," in general terms. The treatment follows immediately on the passage quoted earlier, in which he condemns the supersession by the modern State of "smaller and lower bodies." The Pope gives no technical guidance on his precise conception. He is concerned with three things. That these groups should not be separate for employers and employed; that they should be free, autonomous and spontaneous groups; that the aim is the re-creation of an organic structure of society within the state.

He then devotes a page to a cautious, not to say grudging, analysis of the Fascist form of "corporative organisation." His verdict, even if not unfavourable, is extremely reserved. He notes three points of unsoundness.

"The State is substituting itself in the place of private initiative ... an excessively bureaucratic and political character ... it risks serving particular political aims rather than contributing to the initiation of a better social order."

There is, indeed, a real sense in which the Corporate State is (*a*) a contradiction in terms, because it *imposes* corporations instead of *fostering* them as organic groups, and (*b*) at variance with the principle that the State is an aggregation of families. However that may be, it is clear that the Fascist or other Corporate State may not be adduced as an application of the Encyclical, or as having a specifically Catholic character.

But in certain Catholic quarters which are reluctant to abandon, or even seriously to modify, the methods of industrial production, these references to Vocational Groups have been seized on exclusively as the means of restoring the modern world to justice and order. They have devised as a variant of the "Corporate State," a less rigid "Corporative State." This is becoming as blessed a word as Mesopotamia, for equally indefinite reasons. No self-respecting Catholic Dictator or writer, it appears, may now do other than found or advocate a Corporative State, where Vocational Groups will make all things new.

Three points arise for discussion.

1. We have seen it as an essential feature of Catholic philosophy and the Papal teaching that human welfare proceeds from certain doctrines and institutions *in a given and unchangeable order*.

The modern evils are primarily the depression of Personality and the Family, and the relative absence of the buttress of diffused ownership. When these have been remedied, there arises the wider consideration of larger organic bodies, as the Guild. Clearly, therefore, the establishment of Guilds cannot be instead of, or logically earlier than, the establishment of the antecedent ties, and because the Popes could not be understood, in the face of their clear statement of the due order, to advocate or tolerate such a process of supplanting or elimination, the Vocational Groups may not be adduced as the sole or prior goal to aim at. A certain parallelism may or may not be inevitable in the special urgency of the times. But both the sincerity and the orthodoxy of any proposals must be judged by whether they give due and prior weight to the prior considerations.

2. There is no observable intention that these groups shall raise their members out of their essentially proletarian status. Certainly there is no such process at work in the Italian

Corporations, and with the possible exception of the Portuguese Constitution it does not seem to be in the minds of framers or administrators. A scheme of sharing, while it may partake of the virtues of a temporary expedient, does not of itself affect the proletarian status.

3. There is no visible intention of modifying the industrial processes and organisation in such a way as to remove the damage to integrity inherent in the factory system. Certainly this will not be achieved by any system of profit-sharing, or even of control-sharing, in such a group. In the realm of permanent Catholic principles which are the basis of this essay, a process in this direction would be the first essential. It is considered at greater length in a later chapter, but it is desirable to establish here that no system which declines issue with the abrogation of human responsibility of which the modern factory, under any political system, is the classic expression, can be said to be restoring the permanent Catholic standards to the world.

A society in which any intermediate organic form or institution has been swept away, so that there tend to be only individuals and the State, is tending to the perfection proper to Wasps' or Ants' Nests. This is well in wasps and ants, but not in man, and is the reason why the Papal teaching will not tolerate any supersession of a lower unit. Accordingly, it seems that a collective factory basis cannot be incorporated into the *permanent* Catholic system, for it has superseded a prior form, namely, personal productive property. And it seems to have been overlooked that the tendency to the Wasps' Nest is evident also in the of the collective factory. The point will be elaborated later.

The most that can be hoped from this kind of application of "Vocational Groups" is the decline, and perhaps the elimination, of one type of Captain of Industry. Certainly that would be a gain, and as certainly co-ownership by the workers is more Catholic than the present system.[1] But it is to be hoped that

Catholics who are attempting a step-by-step restoration will not be so ill-advised as to refrain from a full philosophic statement and programme. Otherwise, when the time for the later stages has arrived, it may well be that the Robot will have arrived first, and the pain-nerve be the only hope for reconstruction.

Moreover, it is an incompetence to build on any basis without proving the stability and permanence of that basis. On any showing, the short history of industrialism does not suggest the attributes of permanence or stability. It will be necessary, therefore, for any proposal claiming to base itself on justice, which is eternal, to demonstrate that its equipment has the attribute of permanence to correspond. And if so, it will be necessary to analyse industrialism before deciding, in this sense, on Vocational Groups within its structure.

The Guild to which the Church looks for sanity and dignity in work rests, and must always rest, upon an association of independent integral producers. Without this basis, it may become as easily an instrument of oppression as of betterment; and this for the same reasons as make the possession of productive property essential to full personality and freedom. Perhaps it is of some psychological significance that discussion in English of the "Corporative State" seems instinctively to avoid the use of the word Guild. This is not the place to develop at any length its true features. It may be added, however, that a particular danger surrounds any attempt to give the character of a Guild to an industrial enterprise, without more drastic modification of methods and structure than appears to be envisaged. Fortified as it is necessarily with powers over price and output, it may develop (and has in certain cases developed) an unpleasant form of oppression of the smaller units. No scheme which does not include effective safeguards against

---

[1] But see a further reference to this point in Chapter X.

concealed capitalist buccaneering can fulfil the elementary purpose of a Guild.

III

The development of the concept of the Just Price is one of the greatest glories of the Schoolmen. It is best stated by St. Thomas (2. 2. 77. 1).

"Whatever is established for the common advantage should not be more of a burden to one party than to another, and consequently all contracts between them should observe equality of thing and thing … If either the price exceed the quantity of the thing's worth, or conversely, the thing exceed the price, there is no longer the equality of justice, and consequently to sell a thing for more than it is worth, or to buy it for less than its worth, is in itself unjust and unlawful."

It has been observed by more than one writer that the doctrine of the Just Price presupposes diffused property in society, since this is the only basis that will ensure it.

It was taken to be self-evident that the Just Price could be ascertained and insisted on, and although it would be too much to say that it was universal in the Middle Ages, it is clear that it was very generally achieved. And indeed, in a society where production is direct and personal, and life reasonably simple, the assessment of a Just Price for any article or service is not impossible or difficult, given a body of honest men to forestall the maneuvers of the unscrupulous. In this achievement the Guilds were the chief instrument.

But if the Just Price is the essential basis of Catholic standards of exchange and commerce, then anything which makes the assessment and acceptance of the Just Price difficult or impossible, is to that extent to be discouraged.

The Just Price tends to be a Fixed Price, at any rate in a large society. On the other hand, the Fixed Price is not necessarily a

51

Just Price, and several modern attempts to achieve them have failed for this reason. It is clear that the Just Price involves at least some approximation to simplicity for its establishment. When processes, carriage, selling agencies and other overheads reach a certain complication, the true Just Price has become impossible, and commerce and trade are at once unmoral or immoral. Things sell for what they will fetch, or for what the seller can impose, according to whether competition or monopoly is dominant in the State. It is to this constant bucketing of contrary interests, quite as much as to mechanisation, that the recurrent booms and slumps of industrialism are due. We can only remove such a major growth by a major operation, and an attempt will be made later to assess how radical such an operation must be to restore health to the social body. This is perhaps a suitable point to remind ourselves that are always proportionate to their causes. We have deluded ourselves too long that we could have our cake and eat it. The City of God cannot be brought to pass by a mere change in our methods of book-keeping.

VII: THE STATE

I am the King's good servant, but God's first.—Saint Thomas More.

The State is at once the strongest and the weakest of human institutions. Strongest because largest, weakest because least accessible to the rule of conscience. Provided it does not overstep its bounds, it has always received the warm support of the Church, as being the Vicar of God in human rule.

Unless mankind succeeds in the future in achieving a real Society of Nations, that "Federation of the World" dreamed of by Tennyson and many another, the State is the largest and widest aspect of man's social organisation in the secular sphere. All authority is from God. "Thou shouldst not have any power against Me, unless it were given thee from above." But this has never been taken by the Church to confer any *special* sanctity upon the variants of autocratic or oligarchic rule. She is indifferent to forms of government, unless they invade some prior human right. In a democracy, for example, the people can choose their authority, which thereupon is invested with the attributes of authority. It is true that Christian sentiment has shown great tenderness for monarchical types, chiefly, perhaps, because the person and office of Kingship have been invested with striking forms of unction and consecration. But since it cannot be doubted that Monarchies have often oppressed both the spiritual power and the people, it is clear that no special sanction attaches to them.

Nor can I find anything in the teaching of the Church, and particularly not in St. Thomas, to justify an idea gaining favour in some quarters: the idea that the State is best and most naturally governed by a sort of heritable or co-opted hierarchy of privileged classes. Efforts are made from time to time to show that the basis has Catholic teaching behind it. Usually they are interested efforts. The idea is tolerable, but not specifically Catholic. St. Thomas, for instance, has this striking passage:

"The making of a law belongs either to the whole people, or to a public personage who has care of the whole people."—(2. 1. 90. 3.) Democracy or Monarchy. Oligarchy is not mentioned. The attempts referred to are fittingly reprobated by Maritain in *Freedom in the Modern World*.

The main functions of the State are those which cannot be maintained by the more intimate social units. Defence, the maintenance and perfecting of Distributive Justice, the maintenance of Public Order.

Owing to its peculiar temptations to dominance over and intrusion into matters which are no part of its concern, and to the peculiarly final nature of its sanctions and authority, it is necessary to discuss the limits of State power.

"The end of law," says St. Thomas, "is the common good."—(2. 1. 96. 1.) That is at once its lofty destiny and its limit. Following the Catholic norm, the State has no concern with what may fittingly be carried out by prior authorities.

"Man precedes the State," says Leo XIII in *Rerum Novarum*.

No. 39 of the condemned Propositions in the *Syllabus of Errors* of Pius IX is:

"The State, as the origin and source of all rights, enjoys a right that is unlimited."

Thus the Totalitarian State, whether Communist or Fascist, is not tolerable to Catholic teaching, although in a given case it may be necessary to tolerate it to avoid worse evils. In such cases it is tolerated only pending amelioration by any lawful means.

Apart from Defence, when the imminence of external danger may justify a very wide range of claim on the full service of the citizens (for self-preservation is the primary duty of mankind) the function of the State is carried on chiefly by means of Law.

The concept of Law in St. Thomas is so lofty that he is at pains to preserve us from the tyranny of nominal Law.

"Human Law is law only by virtue of its accordance with right reason: and thus it is manifest that it flows from the eternal law. And in so far as it deviates from right reason it is called an unjust law; in such case it is no law at all, but rather a species of violence."—(2. 1. 93. 3.)

He regards this principle as so important that he gives it more than once, as though to emphasise it by this rare repetition. Thus:

"The force of a law depends on the extent of its justice. Now in human affairs, a thing is said to be just, from being right, according to the rule of reason. But the first rule of reason is the law of nature. ... Consequently every human law has just so much of the nature of law, as it is derived from the law of nature. But if in any point it deflects from the law of nature, it is no longer a law but a perversion of law."—(2. 1. 95. 2.)

Normally, no doubt, the Church would agree that the view of the majority should prevail on any subject competent to it, if it does not bear on any natural right. But Leo XIII warns us that this rule of the majority is not unlimited:

"Hence the doctrine of the supremacy of the greater number, and that all right and all duty reside in the majority. But from what has been said it is clear that all this is in contradiction to reason."—(*Libertas Præstantissimum.*)

It is clear, then, that right reason is the norm of law, and therefore of the authority of the State.

For a nation is happy when its citizens are happy. What else is a nation but a number of men living in concord?"—(St. Augustine, Ep ad Maced: c. iii.)

Provided that society is organic, and the hierarchy of human institutions are in their right order and vigour, it may be said that that State is best governed which is least governed. For clearly a State in which Persons and Families have due dignity and are "contented with their own," and in which Guilds and other organic bodies enrich the common life, the State will need to intervene only in exception and in emergency.

But in Modern Times, Industrial Capitalism has so stripped social life of its organisms and safeguards as to set up violent movements of action and reaction.

The Masters of Industrialism have on the one hand absorbed most of the social buttresses, leaving "a dust of individuals," on the other, as the Popes have recorded with indignation, they have usurped the functions of the State.

"The fierce battle to acquire control of the State, so that its resources and authority may be abused in the economic struggles. ... The State which should be the supreme arbiter, ruling in kingly fashion far above all party contention, intent only upon justice and the common good, has become instead a slave, bound over to the service of human passion and greed."— (*Quadragesimo Anno.*)

Capitalism first monopolised the State in order to prevent and forestall any State action, not only for the restoration of justice, but for the amelioration of the lot of the poor and dispossessed. The disgraceful details of this period are sufficiently well known to enable any discussion to be dispensed with here. But when this process has continued to a certain point, both the resources and the functions of the various organisms have become so exhausted or atrophied that to prevent a complete collapse the State must intervene more and more largely, with the result, as we see to-day, that the most elementary personal, familial and Guild rights and duties are taken over by the State. This in turn, after a period of short-sighted opposition by the rich, leads to a further step on the downward path, the establishment of that Servile State whose essence and danger have been set before us so conclusively by Mr. Belloc.

Once this process has passed a certain point, the ideological concept of the State as the source and dispenser of all good and right is bound to emerge. It exists, without avowal or definite philosophy, in England. It has reached its frankest avowal in the Totalitarian States. Their claims have been attacked vigorously by the present Pontiff:

"And here we find ourselves confronted by a mass of authentic affirmations, and no less authentic facts which reveal beyond the slightest possibility of doubt the resolve (already in great measure actually put into effect) to monopolise completely the young, from their tenderest years up to manhood and womanhood, for the exclusive advantage of a party and of a régime based on an ideology, which clearly resolves itself into a true, a real pagan worship of the State—the "Statolatry" which is no less in contrast with the natural rights of the family than it is in contradiction with the supernatural rights of the Church.

"A conception of the State which makes the rising generations belong to it entirely, without any exception, from the tenderest years up to adult life, cannot be reconciled by a Catholic either with Catholic doctrine or with the natural rights of the family. It is not possible for a Catholic to accept the claim that the Church and the Pope must limit themselves to the external practices of religion (such as Mass and the Sacraments) and that all the rest of education belongs to the State."—(*Non Abbiamo Bisogno.*)

"Whoever exalts race, or the people, or the State, or a particular form of State, or the depositaries of power, or any other fundamental value of the human community—however necessary and honourable be their function in worldly things— whoever raises these notions above their standard value and divinises them to an idolatrous level, distorts and perverts an order of the world planned and created by God."—(*Mit Brennender Sorge.*)

The State is faced to-day, therefore, with a task of peculiar delicacy and extent. It has to take the initiative in restoring social justice and the norms of organic right, involving action of a specially drastic kind; and it must do this with the sole and single-minded intention of abrogating all its intimate control once these organisms are viable and the just basis restored. In both these divisions of the task Catholics, with their unique standards of right reason and right living, will have to play a decisive part. There is all the more need for them not to be drawn to Right or Left in their concept of social life. Otherwise the very urgency of the danger will ensure its permanence.

It would take us far beyond the limits of this little book to attempt to discuss the line and scope proper to this action. But one principle may be indicated.

The State can absorb or it can foster. If the former, it will proceed by taking over, in direct or indirect fashion, the whole conduct of the institution it desires to set up. Of this type are the Agricultural Marketing Boards, actual or proposed, in England, which take in their stride the setting up of such things as butter and bacon factories, egg grading and marketing stations, and so on, all on the grandiose scale which is associated with mass production. Every gallon of milk sold in England is passed through the books of Milk Marketing Board as a middle-man.

The very scale of the units and schemes will preclude their resumption at a later date by "the smaller units" stipulated by the Pope. Among other results will be the stabilising and making permanent the very excess of industrialisation (culminating in a strictly communistic basis) which has brought them into being.

If the State is to *foster* the re-creation of Guilds, it will act quite differently. It will lay down a framework of such a nature as will promote spontaneous groups of adequate but not excessive size, locally controlled so far as circumstances permit. It will fix statutory prices, and the operation of the interests of producer and consumer will ensure that they are maintained. In particular it will lay down a framework of rules to favour local against bureaucratic organisation, and to favour small producers as against large, since that is the prime need for the whole process.

From such a framework the State can retire with dignity and satisfaction when the system has shown itself to be viable.

VIII: THE SOCIAL ORDER ENVISAGED BY THE CHURCH

You are the Salt of the earth, but if the salt have lost its savour, with what shall it be salted?
—Matt. v, 13.

We are now in a position to form a definite idea of the essential structure of the society which would correspond as a whole with the requirements of Catholic Social Teaching.

From the conclusions already arrived at in the preceding chapters such a structure will have to conform to the following principles :

1. Its substance must be consonant throughout to the Natural Law and therefore to justice.
2. Its parts and its whole must not only be integral and just, they must maintain a certain due order and function from the primary upwards and from the intimate outwards.
3. It must not be hostile or unfavourable at any point to the nature of man. Any doubtful point must be referred always to that nature, and not to any other principle.
4. The Church attaches primary importance to the principle that a Person or Family should have control of his or its environment, at least in so far as that environment is necessary to the full development of personal or family functions.

All these points are indisputable in the light of the body of doctrine already quoted, but it may be desirable to offer here some little amplification of the last of them.

Control in human affairs can usually only be effective when it is direct. For as in human affairs all the effective agents are human, indirect control involves a human chain of causality. Now "whenever in a chain of causality there occurs a human will, the effects which follow are mediate and not immediate."[2]

That is to say, as all human wills are free, a contact between a person and some necessary or requisite good, if it depend on a chain of intervening human agents, can only be contingent. Or in words even plainer, no man can be sure of receiving or possessing anything over which his control is not immediate. And this is valid in the political, the social, the legal, the economic and the geographic sense.

But so far as the good is necessary the person cannot be content with contingent control, and neither can the Church be content that such control is contingent. Therefore, to the extent that a good is necessary, and with diminishing force as the good recedes towards the status of a mere convenience or luxury, the Church would insist on the direct in society as against the indirect. It is desirable to add that this notion of directness involves also an approximation to *simplicity*. But simplicity is not *inadequacy*, as so many moderns absurdly suppose. Its contrary is *complexity*. Other things being equal, complexity is a disadvantage or even an evil, and simplicity a good; for all the great human goods are of their nature simple, and therefore complexity recedes from good as it recedes from simplicity.

The structure we are to consider will have all the force of a diagram or skeleton. It may not have the force of a picture or a portrait. The Church lays down principles. Their application is normally the function of society at large. In the case of Moral Theology, the principles have been worked out in such detail that it may be said to approach the character of a portrait. In social

---

[2] I owe this luminous phrasing of a permanent principle of logic to Father Vincent McNabb. He made it seventeen years ago in poignant circumstances which did him great honour.

matters, the working out has been complete chiefly in their negative aspect, as the lower limit of tolerability approaches the region of sin. In its positive aspects, the working out is left to society and is necessarily less precise. Thus the present Pope, in his Apostolic Letter to Mexico of Lent 1937, has this passage: "Catholic Action should never take responsibility in matters that are purely technical, financial or economic, because such matters lie outside the scope and purpose of Catholic Action." But evidently this is said in the narrowest technical sense, for in his letter to the Cardinal Archbishop of Breslau, the Pope says: "We are speaking of an Action which embraces the *whole* man, and which aims at his integral civic and religious formation. … It embraces societies and of every kind, whether they be for the promotion of piety, the formation of the young, or for a strictly social or economic end."

Since from the negative we may usually deduce at least the form of the positive, and since in their lengthy analyses of society Popes and Doctors have been bound to present as complete a picture as possible, we are able with confidence to deduce not only the skeleton, but sufficient of the lineaments to make a recognisable figure. To this delineation we shall now proceed.

Firstly: "For imperfect happiness such as can be had in this life, external goods are necessary, not as belonging to the essence of happiness, but by serving as instruments to happiness, which consists in an operation of virtue as stated in *Ethic* 1. For man needs in this life the necessaries of the body, both for the operation of contemplative virtue, and for the operation of active virtue, for which latter he needs also many other things by means of which to perform its operations."—(St. Thomas 2. 1. 4. 7.)

The human person is born into a world capable of furnishing him with a full range of instruments to enable him to maintain and to perfect his personality, and to achieve his destiny of human happiness on earth and perfect happiness in God. Such range of instruments is *owed* to man by Nature, that is, by God, and consists first of a sufficiency of things, second of the principles for speculative and practical reason, and third of the spiritual succours, culminating in those of the Catholic Church.

The assets of mankind are normally made available by work expended on natural resources. This is the method ordained by Almighty God to keep man's faculties, so to speak, in condition.

The recognition, by himself and by society, of his self-subsistent personality, that is of his power to act *of his own right*, is the basis of all human action.

This recognition excludes the domination of other human wills in any matter essential to his personal status. It includes the right to property, the right to marriage and the right to form his familial and social contacts without let or hindrance.

His property is of a kind and extent which assures to him the performance of all his essential functions as Person, Husband and Father. Therefore it is adequate to support a family in human dignity and sufficiency. Its extent varies with period, climate and local natural resources, but there is a certain amplitude below which it cannot fall.

The limitations of human energy impose a natural term to the extent to which a given person can command immediate control over all his wants. Hence the material need, which is the primary need, for social life. But the more such control is over his primary needs the more it is in accord with Catholic concepts.

Since the primary human needs are food, clothing, shelter and fuel, in that order, the husbandman is the classic independent Person and closest to the Catholic concept, for in husbandry all these essential goods are under immediate control. And moreover human work is dignified in proportion to its necessity. It is necessary for a husbandman to be in immediate physical contact with his land.

The next most perfect setting for the Person is that of the

Craftsman in necessary works. The maker of primary tools, the builder of houses, the weaver, the maker of furniture. By the imperious need of the maximum of directness in human relations, so that chains of causality are as short as possible, these craftsmen are in immediate contact with the husbandmen in communities as small as is consistent with adequacy. Hence the village, held in neighbourly bonds. Within these limits, the aim of an individual person will not be the greatest production of one article or part of an article, but the widest *range* of production to the limit of his ability. The craftsman, for example, will normally also cultivate land on a more modest scale.

Since an essential function of the family is the education of children, and since education means education for life, that society is more perfect where both parents are normally available to guide, encourage or check the offspring, and where the equipment of the household is such as to afford the widest range to such education. Hence domestic production is in full accord with the mind of the Church, and separate and distant production, as in the large towns of industrialism, recedes from it.

Since there are human needs whose incidence is relatively rare, and goods and services which, though infrequent, demand a high skill, the village is supplemented by the occasional town. Within due limits, the relative remoteness of these towns from contact with the primaries will be compensated for by the wider opportunities of a specific type of culture. Such towns should never exceed the limits of organic growth. Once they do, they have lost their sanction.

It is a contravention of due order for the larger body to usurp the functions of the smaller, and therefore a town should not centralise within itself goods and services which can be supplied adequately by the village or the family. Conversely, but in a vaguer sense, the village should not seek to forestall the necessary services of the town.

Nothing in this system should constrain the citizens to do that for which they lack the power. As St. Thomas says: "No man is bound to the impossible: wherefore no man sins by omission, if he does not do what he cannot."—(2. 2. 79. 3 ad 2.)

Thus the responsibility of property is not forced on a man who by defect of qualities cannot sustain it. There will be scope for the servant in any community. It is doubtful, however, whether a refusal to accept this responsibility is justified if it arises from laziness or unwillingness in the head of a family, for he has assumed the responsibility of a family, and "in no other way" can he fulfil his duties to his offspring but by the control of property.

The whole community will use its work as a means of sanctification and development of personality:

"But they shall strengthen the state of the world: and their prayer shall be in the work of their craft, applying their soul, and searching in the law of the Most High."—(Ecclus. 38. 39.)

That this is no fanciful picture will be evident, not only from what I hope is its close adherence to the principles already discussed, but from the picture given by one of the greatest Doctors of the Church; when he turned his mind to such a concrete discussion.

The passages are confined to their present length only from considerations of space.

"Now there are two ways in which an abundance of food stuffs can be supplied to a city. The first we have already mentioned, where the soil is so fertile that it nobly provides for all the necessities of human life. The second is by trade, through which the necessaries of life are brought to the town from different places. But it is quite clear the first means is better. For the higher a thing is the more self-sufficient it is; since whatever needs another's help is by that fact proven inferior. But that city is more fully self-sufficient which the surrounding country supplies with all its vital needs, than is another which must obtain these supplies by trade. A city which has an abundance of food from its own territory, is more dignified than one which is provisioned by merchants. It is safer, too, it seems, for the importing of supplies can easily be prevented whether owing to the uncertain outcome of wars or to the many dangers of the road, and thus the city may be overcome through lack of food.

****

"Again, if the citizens themselves devote their lives to matters of trade, the way will be opened to many vices. For since the object of trading leads especially to making money, greed is awakened in the hearts of the citizens through the pursuit of trade. The result is that everything in the city will be offered for sale: confidence will be destroyed and the way opened to all kinds of trickery: each one will work only for his own profit, despising the public good: the cultivation of virtue will fail, since honour, virtue's reward, will be bestowed upon anybody. Thus, in such a city civic life will necessarily be corrupted. Consequently, the perfect city will make a moderate use of merchants.

****

"Finally that state enjoys a greater measure of peace whose people are more sparsely assembled together and dwell in smaller proportion within the walls of the town. For when men are crowded together, it is an occasion of quarrels and all the elements for seditious plots are provided. Whence, according to Aristotle, it is more profitable to have the people engaged outside the cities than for them to dwell continually within the walls."— (St. Thomas Aquinas, *De Regimine Principium*.)

In their more formal aspects, the questions of commerce are discussed more fully in a later chapter. For our present purpose it is necessary only to round off our picture by consideration of other points arising from human society.

The best basis for a true social life is the association of equals in whom personality has been developed by control of a sufficiency of things. On any other basis it must have a note of febrile refuge in some form of unreality or degradation. Only balanced and dignified work leads to balanced and dignified leisure. Accordingly, the community we are considering will be extremely rich in organic groups such as Craft, Social and Recreational Guilds.

In such a community, unhampered by excessive taxation or imposts of the rich, the amount of leisure available will be ample without being excessive, and it will permit of a full social life. The evidence of such communities is available and adequate. Where work in them is unduly arduous it is found invariably that the bureaucrat, the usurer, or other oppressor has been at work.

Man is to sanctify himself by work suited to his dignity and nature. The Leisure State is un-Catholic and unreasonable. Too much and too constant work brutalises a man. Too much and too constant leisure dissipates and degrades him. The evidence afforded by the leisured classes of history is conclusive on the point. There is no reason to suppose that leisured people from the working classes will do better with their lives than leisured people who have inherited their capacity for leisure and may be said to have been trained for it. On the whole, their time is either frittered away in conventional posturing or frivolous or degrading pleasures, or they seek to use their leisure to control the lives of others. Of the two the former is the less dangerous and disgusting, but neither is to be sought for on Catholic or other grounds. It cannot be doubted that the general hankering after leisure which is a mark of industrialised societies is an instinctive reaction against degraded forms of work and would be relatively absent from a sounder society.

There is much evidence that after the discipline of sound

work, a reasonable amount of leisure is used for decent recreation and culture. There is no evidence that excessive leisure will have anything but a corrupting or that it will be otherwise used. With a gravity unusual even in a Papal document Leo XIII warned us against the Leisure State:

"If any there are who pretend differently—who hold out to a hard-pressed people the boon of freedom from pain and trouble, an undisturbed repose, and constant enjoyment—they delude the people and impose upon them, and their lying promises will only one day bring forth evils worse than the present."—(*Rerum Novarum.*)

If the brief sketch I have ventured to make here has obvious affinities with certain types of society in the past, and other types which still flourish in the modern world, that is not the concern of the present writer. So far as our human experience goes, it is this type of society which conforms as a whole to Catholic teaching. I submit that the correspondence is too close to be accidental. Other forms may approximate to it, or be tolerable. This alone fulfils the Law. I do not exclude the possibility that other types, so far untried, may be found in the future to comply with the Catholic requirements. So far they do not exist and have not been outlined. Certainly, at hardly any point is the present system coincident, and those points are so fragmentary as to afford no basis for a sound edifice.

But from this very circumstance my readers may conclude that the task of Catholicising society is too massive even to be attempted, much less to be achieved. It would be a pity if such a counsel of despair were to succeed. Certainly the difficulties are very great, and it cannot be doubted that humanly speaking some major catastrophe, due to the enormous modern affronts to justice and nature, will have to prelude a reaction on an adequate scale. I propose to deal with the subject more at length in my final chapter, but here I would suggest the outline of the argument for hope.

Formidable as it is, the task of social reconstruction fades into insignificance before two other human conflicts. I mean the elimination of slavery and war. The first has been achieved, and achieved, as the Popes have always claimed, by the operation of Catholic principles. At any moment during that process it must inevitably have seemed a hopeless task. Yet it succeeded. Slavery will return only by our own fault.

The elimination of war has not reached the same happy end, but it would be unduly pessimistic not to see, despite much evidence to the contrary, a slow movement of massive will towards this great goal. Its chief impediment is precisely the capitalist industrialism to which we now turn.

So it is with Social Justice. There is a great body of opinion all over the world which would see willingly the supersession of capitalist industrialism. Nothing happens, because it is precisely capitalist industrialism, with its brutal greed and which is ruling the world. But that is only food for hope. Slavery ceased although it was of the very structure of society, and no man dared to challenge it directly.

Industrialism is not of the very structure of society. It is recent and it has no philosophy. Many are challenging it.

Pour vaincre que faut-il? De l'audace! Et encore de l'audace! Et toujours de l'audace! Et le monde est sauvé! ["To vanquish the enemy…we must have audacity, still more audacity, always audacity… and the world will be saved."]

IX: THE CONTRAST OF INDUSTRIALISM

My son, in thy lifetime be not indigent, for it is better to die than to want. The life of him that looketh towards another man's table is not to be counted a life; for he feedeth his soul with another man's meat.—Ecclus. xl, 29,30.

Woe to you that join houst to house and lay field to field, even to the end of the place: shall you alone dwell in the midst of the earth?—Isaias v, 8.

Industrialism is that form of production in bulk which operates by subdivision and segregation of processes in making and distributing things.

Up to the present its form has been Capitalist, but there is no obstacle to a full Industrialism on a Communist-Fascist basis. That, indeed, is its logical end, as many of the most intelligent writers on the subject have perceived.

In *either* form, it is essentially materialist and therefore anti-Catholic, for it makes dignity in work impossible and substitutes a kind of "greed of gain" for the organic connection between man and his work, by imposing indifference to the actual work and substituting labour as an unpleasant preliminary to the real life of leisure hours, if any.

In *either* form, it affronts Catholic principles by making impossible personal control of the necessary minimum of things.

In its Capitalist form, it has always imposed insufficiency and insecurity on the bulk of its personnel, and intends to continue doing so, for work under Industrialism is so repugnant and uninteresting that only "the fear of the sack" will ensure a supply of labour. In its Collectivist form, *other things being equal* (which they are not), it is slightly less intolerable to Catholic principles, for at least the intention is to divide up the total product with some regard to fairness.

Clearly it has two main aspects: as a social system, and as a determinant of the lives of individual persons. Although they are in contact at almost all points, it will be necessary to treat them separately, for the sake of simplicity. Accordingly the effect of Industrialism on individual persons will be discussed chiefly in the next chapter.

Industrialism is bound almost from its origins, and irrevocably, to the machine. It is true that at the very end of the pre-machinery age, the highly capitalist eighteenth century made an attempt to exploit human labour by that subdivision of processes which is characteristic of Industrialism. Adam Smith and his pin are the classic example. But this was relatively restricted, and it seems clear that such processes would have remained restricted but for the advent of the god out of the machine. As a feature or a determinant of social life Industrialism came in with mechanisation.

Everywhere it has imposed a like form on society. It has drawn property into huge aggregations owned by a small minority of the community. Even where, in small ineffective blocks, it is still owned more widely, the sole control is in the hands of such a small minority, who may or may not be the same persons as own the large aggregations. It has drawn population into huge aggregations of unprecedented size. There is no parallel in history to industrial towns like London, New York or Berlin. It has imposed on social life, all over the world in which it operates, a monotony and standardisation terrifying to anyone who grasps the essential richness and variety of human powers. It has imposed, and is imposing, a physical and spiritual sterility on mankind.

That is, it is destructive of human personality.

It has almost no redeeming features, as will be seen.

It is true that a few of the more intelligent Industrialists, notably Mr. Henry Ford, have seen the pit of annihilation before them, and have advanced proposals for splitting up details of their production into small units placed in the countrysides. But clearly this will be ineffectual for two reasons. The extreme sub-division of work carried out by Mr. Ford cannot be made more dignified in a field than in Detroit, nor can its spiritual effect be evaded there. Therefore he will corrupt the countrysides without saving the persons who are bound to him. Moreover, this is only physically possible with some few and minor details of his processes. Much of the heavier and more complicated production, and all the assembly, must remain centralised.

The Popes have shown great uneasiness over two aspects of Industrialism in particular: First its despotism and materialism. There is the classic phrase beginning:

"A small number of very rich men" (Leo XIII). The position having worsened in this respect by 1931, the strictures of Pius XI are more pointed and severe:

"The regulations legally enacted for corporations, with their divided responsibility and limited liability, have given rise to abominable abuses."

"The few who hold excessive wealth and the many who live in destitution, constitute a grave evil in modern society."

"It is patent that in our days, not alone is wealth accumulated, but immense power and despotic economic domination is concentrated in the hands of a few."

"Unbridled ambition for domination has succeeded the desire for gain."

"Grasping, as it were, in their hands the very soul of production, so that no one dare breathe against their will."—(*Quadragesimo Anno.*)

But stern as are these words, they are equalled or surpassed by others which indicate the affronts to human dignity involved in the system.

"Or degraded them with conditions repugnant to their dignity as human beings. … No man may with impunity outrage that human dignity which God Himself has treated with reverence.—(*Rerum Novarum.*)

"How universally has the true Christian spirit become impaired, which formerly produced such lofty sentiments even in uncultured and illiterate men! In its stead, man's one solicitude is to obtain his daily bread in any way he can. And so bodily labour, which was decreed by Providence for the good of man's body and soul even after original sin, has everywhere been changed into an instrument of strange perversion; for dead matter leaves the factory ennobled and transformed, where men are corrupted and degraded."—(*Quadragesimo Anno.*)

For some reason which escapes me, it is sometimes assumed that such passages as these refer only to low wages or moral conditions. There seems no reason to assume that when the Popes say human dignity, they do not mean human dignity in all its aspects, and especially in the most vital of them.[3]

The most obvious vice of Industrialism is its inability, up to the present, to concede a decent standard of life to the bulk of the workers. It has never conceded, for example, a family wage, and whether this is actually possible or not, it seems to have been overlooked that the expedient of "Family Allowances" really implies the bankruptcy of the system. It is not without interest that to many reformers Industrialism is still the Promised Land in spite of its history of unrelieved squalor and oppression of the poor.

The methods of Industrialised production and their effect on

---

[3] A distinguished non-Catholic economist, Werner Sombart, in A New Social Philosophy takes it for granted that the passage quoted from Quadragesimo Anno is in condemnation of Industrialism as such.

the victims of the system will be discussed in the next chapter, and the failure of Industrialism to implement happiness and sufficiency or the organic life is so notorious that it need not be amplified at this point.

It is necessary, however, to abstract from what may be merely temporary, even if there be no evidence of it, and to consider the matter more radically. If this book were excluding morals and salvation from its consideration, the undoubted fact that Industrialism, or more properly *urbanisation*, has an attraction for modern man would be important. But to a system which has always insisted that happiness follows from right action, and that man ought to do what he ought to do, and not merely what he wants to do, the fact is irrelevant. For *if* Industrialism is hostile to the nature, welfare and real destiny of man, the official exponents of Catholic doctrine are bound to dissuade Catholics from it as definitely as from any other occasion of sin. The plea that "they prefer it" would be as absurd as the plea that they preferred fornication to chastity.

But on the whole, it is not true that this attraction has any greater force than that of a will o' the wisp. Simple souls are attracted by the bright lights. Once in the lights they cannot find their way without guidance out into the healing dark. Those whose families have been in the machine for generations have had hitherto no real conception, and certainly no object-lesson or experience, of any alternative. Naturally they follow normal human practice in trying to make the best of their lot. But as cheerfulness and humour in the trenches were no justification for trench warfare, so resignation in Industrialism cannot be urged in favour of inaction.

This vice of *illusion* runs through any life which is bound to Industrialism. A prevalence of illusion means a powerful subconscious impulse to escape. Consider, for example, industrial recreations. They are athletic games (largely vicarious) which are themselves an important sense a substitute for facing up to reality. But this is the more dignified form. The others are Newspapers, the Wireless and the Cinema. All of them are illusions of illusions.

Let us turn to the avowed case for Industrialism. I say the avowed case, because the real case is not avowable, being based entirely on avarice. It might have been that machines were initiated for some great good, as to drain a marsh. But the Dutch Engineers brought the Fens to their highest state of cultivability with no other machinery than windmills. No modern achievement under Industrialism surpasses this, even in mere scale and difficulty. Machines were in fact introduced to enable capitalists to make more and easier money. Until recently no serious attempt was made to invoke any higher motive. But with the advent of certain panaceas, themselves made necessary by the very existence of Industrialism, there has arisen a conviction that we can eat our cake and have it. That we can delete *Capitalist* and retain *Industrialist* with profit to all concerned. Their slogan is "The Age of Plenty."

We have to consider, therefore, two things. Does Industrialism give an age of plenty and does it offer permanence?

St. Thomas, in considering avarice, gives us this illuminating principle. "It is directly a sin against one's neighbours, because in exterior things one man cannot have superabundance without another being in want, since temporal goods cannot simultaneously be possessed by many." (II. II. 118. 1. ad 2.)

St. Thomas took it as self-evident that the totality of human goods could not exceed a certain maximum. Up to the present, it remains limited, as is shown by the co-existence of wealth and destitution. Has Industrialism, in its essence, invalidated this assumption? The modern world unhesitatingly says yes. "Thus can be achieved the great necessity of steadily and systematically increasing the power to consume as science and rationalisation increase the power to produce."—(Mosley. *Greater Britain*, p. 100.) This is quoted as being typical of what every "modernist" holds. The principle is imposed upon anyone who retains Industrialism in his Utopia.

But is it true or possible? In two ways it can be shown to be false and suicidal. Eight years ago, the point was discussed at length by Commander Herbert Shove in *The Fairy Ring of Commerce*.[4] Its thesis has never been contested.

Material resources are of two kinds, replaceable and irreplaceable. The replaceables are organic products, the results of the seasonal growth of crops. The irreplaceables are inorganic, such as minerals. Nature imposes an immovable limit to the increase of organic products, because these are *seasonal*, and no conceivable scientific method can remove this obstacle. In past times society was normally organic in all its aspects, because the production of organic goods kept perfect pace with the production by direct craft methods of inorganic goods.

As soon as machine production passed a certain modest point, a condition of strain or duality was set up. Machinery itself operates to a surprising extent on organic material. Fast machine weaving has a limit because wool and cotton are organic and cannot be multiplied quickly or indefinitely.

Rubber is an organic product which imposes a practical limit on transport. Machine saw-mills, furniture factories and newspapers depend on forests for their continuance, and so on. Where the material is inorganic, as in iron and steel, the supply is immediately available, but irreplaceable.

Now high Industrialism has only proceeded up to the present, and can only proceed in the future, by :

(a) setting up a condition of intense strain as between itself

---

[4] Now unfortunately out of print. I hope a second edition may soon be possible.

and agriculture, due to the tremendous difference in *tempo*.

(b) Invading ruthlessly our capital stocks of irreplaceable raw material.

Such is the thesis.

Thus the achievements of Industrialism. Its meritricious brilliance, the apparent ease with which it satiates the material desires of man, are due solely to living on capital.

Only in a world dominated and silenced by greed could this enormous fact have been concealed. For terrifying things have happened already, and more terrifying things impend.

1. It has been estimated that the destruction of the world's forests has proceeded with such ghastly and wanton speed that after only about fifty years of it, we are within twenty-five years of exhaustion. Forests are organic, but they were the product of ages. In no practical sense can they be said to be replaceable on the Industrial scale.

2. Petrol and Paraffin have been used so recklessly that some authorities claim to see the end of this irreplaceable commodity within half a century. No one knows what untried resources there may be, but with half the millionaires in the world hunting for them they cannot be very numerous! To resort to spirit produced by vegetation is only to trespass on a field which the world will need for food.

3. By ruthless single-cropping for industry, the cotton areas of America are within sight of exhaustion. More serious still, a great part of the Middle Western basin of America, for the same reason, has *disappeared* as a food-producing area. Its soil, reduced to dust by constant "Wheat-mining," blew across the continent into the Atlantic in 1936. An increasing area in Canada is faced with the same fate.

This has been one of the great disasters of history. Its scale is almost beyond belief. But as my friend K. L. Kenrick said recently, "We did not realise that Capitalism was prepared to destroy the human race in order to save itself." A few brief words in the Press, and silence kept the ring for the next disaster. Presumably Australia and the Argentine, as the chief remaining one-crop areas of the world, will be the next to blow up in dust.

No one knows how near or how far may be the exhaustion of other raw materials, but it is clear they are exhaustible.

Therefore a system which operates by so drastic and wanton an invasion of our capital resources is condemned by all human standards, and the "Age of Plenty" must go down the wind with the soil of the Middle West.

Moreover, the Age of Plenty is doubtful on internal. grounds. There is no opportunity to develop the thesis at length, but it is clear that under any political system Industrialism tends In nullify its own productive powers by multiplying and creating a mass of new functions in planning, transporting, maintaining, advertising and selling and other unproductive "overheads."

A glance at the staggering proportions of clerical and distributing personnel will make this clear. The population, aged 14 and over, of England and Wales is shown in the 1931 census as 31,043,753.

An analysis, by allocation of the "gainful occupations" into Productive and Unproductive Groups, gives the following results. As this is not a Statistical Survey, they have been shown to the nearest hundred thousand for the sake of simplicity.

[See table on page 80]

Agriculture	1,200,000		
Mining	1,000,000		
Other Production and Assembly	5,800,000	Total Productive Population, including Assembly	8,000,000
Transport, Packing, etc.	2,200,000		
Insurance, Finance, Commerce	2,100,000		
Clerks and Typists	1,400,000		
Servants and Entertainers	2,500,000		
State and Professions	1,000,000	Total Population in Unproductive Occupations	9,200,000
Married Women, Retired Persons and Passengers	13,800,000		13,800,000
	31,000,000		31,000,000

(Census of England and Wales, 1931. Occupation Tables, pp. 1-15, H.M.S.O., 1934.)

It will be agreed that the proportions are astonishing. A closer analysis is unnecessary for the present purpose, but it is clear that the proportion of unproductive to productive occupation is increasing steadily.

I need not discuss the obvious fact that the great bulk of these unproductive operations partake of the nature of industrialism proper, especially in their high sub-division and remoteness from reality. An increasing amount of mechanisation in the form of calculating machines and typewriters is also taking its toll of the personnel in these fields.

The census grouping has been followed, but two circumstances make the real disproportion more striking even than is shown in the figures. Printing and Electricity, for example, are allocated entirely to the Production Group, although both are largely of an unproductive nature.

Moreover, the personnel of each category in the Productive Group includes functions which are unproductive.

The largest towns in the world are not productive, but parasitic. London and New York consist chiefly of salesmen and clerks. We do not realise, although the evidence confronts us every day, what a high proportion of industrial production is for mere transport and maintenance of the system itself. I commend a scrutiny of these proportions to my readers. I commend to them also the fact that in machine production material tends more and more to be impermanent and rubbishy. Necessarily so, because really permanent materials deserve and frequently admit the dignity of working by hand.

But there is a defect more fundamental still. Industrialism has destroyed the organic society. It is now destroying the very physical and mental basis of permanence.

The family life went long since. The very ability to make a family, as well as the will, is now going. For it seems clear that infertility is now becoming involuntary as well as voluntary.

This is a feature of Industrialism which demands separate and lengthy treatment. The fact is undoubted. Survival rates all over the industrial world are below unity. That is, populations are not only not increasing, they are of failing to reproduce themselves. Our own in England is down to 73 per cent. of unity. It is slightly higher in America at present, but that is only because the average age is lower. In all essentials the prospects are the same.

The problem his been observed with anxiety in many quarters. Even the Federation of British Industries has seen it. But in more disinterested quarters discussion has been more fruitful.

We may select for quotation a recent work by Dr. Alexis Carrel of the Rockefeller Institute—*Man the Unknown.* Dr. Carrel is one of the world's great biologists, and one of the great scientists assembled by the present Pope in the Papal Academy of Science, and his lengthy discussion of why Industrialism is destroying mankind should be read by anyone who wishes to form an intelligent opinion on the subject.

His technical chapters are naturally unsuitable for reproduction, but a few of his conclusions may be given here.

"Men cannot follow modern civilisation along its present course, because they are degenerating. They have been fascinated by the beauty of sciences of inert matter. They have not understood that their body and consciousness are subjected to natural laws, more obscure than, but as inexorable as the laws of the sidereal world. Neither have they understood that they cannot transgress these laws without being punished."

"The response of the women to the modifications brought about in the ancestral habits by industrial civilisation has been immediate and decisive. The birth-rate has at once fallen."

"Modern life is opposed to the life of the mind."

"Wealth is as dangerous as ignorance and poverty … We

need a way of life involving constant struggle, mental and muscular physiological and moral discipline, and some privations."

"Most civilised men manifest only an elementary form of consciousness. They are capable of the easy work which in modern society insures the survival of the individual. They produce, they consume, they satisfy their physiological appetites. They also take pleasure in watching, among great crowds, athletic spectacles, in seeing childish and vulgar moving pictures, in being rapidly transported without effort, or in looking at swiftly moving objects. They are soft, sentimental, lascivious, and violent. They have no moral, esthetic, or religious sense."

"Despite the marvels of scientific civilisation, human personality tends to dissolve."

"Certain forms of modern life lead directly to degeneration. There are social conditions as fatal to white men as are warm and humid climates. We react to poverty, anxieties and sorrows by working and struggling. We can stand tyranny, revolution and war. But we are not able to fight successfully against misery or prosperity. The individual and the race are weakened by extreme poverty. Wealth is just as dangerous."

"Men would live in small communities instead of in immense droves... The peasant owning his land, the fisherman owning his boat, although obliged to work hard, are nevertheless masters of themselves and of their time. Most industrial workers could enjoy similar independence and dignity. ...

"It seems that modern business organisation and mass-production are incompatible with the full development of the human self. If such is the case, then industrial civilisation, and not civilised man, must go."

"The development of human personality, is the ultimate purpose of civilisation."

I quote so extensively from Dr. Carrel not only because of

his eminence, but because he has dealt formally with what many philosophers and scientists are expressing by passages of incidental anxiety. Mr. Aldous Huxley, Professor J. B. S. Haldane, and Lord Horder, may be mentioned as distinguished cases in point.

But if even a part of this indictment be true, Industrialism is no proper basis for a system which must last to the end of the world. It is time we began to react with the Popes.

NOTE.—After the completion of this book there was published an important work on agriculture—"Famine in England," by Viscount Lymington. (Witherby, London, 7s. 6d.)

This eminent authority on agriculture deals formally and at length with the destruction, actual or impending, of the food-producing areas of the world as the direct result of the demands and methods of Industrialism. In particular he endorses and gives detailed evidence for much of the argument developed in the foregoing chapter. "Europe already cannot supply her own needs, and the world, which a decade ago seemed limitless, is contracting like a sucked orange before our eyes" (p. 106).

X: WORK AND THE MACHINE

All these will I give Thee if, falling down, Thou wilt adore me.
—Matt. iv, 9.

Now the reason in the craftsman's mind about the thing to be made is art: therefore the philosopher says (6 Ethic) that art is right reason about things to be made.—St. Thomas. *Contra Gentiles* 93.

We are now to consider Work and the Machine, and therefore workmen and machinists. It is difficult to approach the subject without anger, so "Isolated and helpless" have been the victims of industrialism. Nearly fifty years ago, Cardinal Manning's compassion said of them:

"So dependent upon the will of the rich, so exposed to the fluctuations of adversity, and to the vicissitudes of trade." And there was no Bedaux System, no Assembly Belt, and no Automatic Lathe or Press, in Cardinal Manning's day.

Art, as we have seen above, is right reason about things to be made. Not some remote and ineffectual talent which needs a studio and a Bohemian life for its practice. Mr. Eric Gill, with his double authority as a philosopher and a master-craftsman, has exposed that nonsense for many years. "an artist is not a special kind of man, but every man is a special kind of artist." Art, in other words, is *human work*, if by human we mean the full concurrence of the faculties of man in the task. He must have strength and skill. He must also have an intellectual concept of the thing to be made. And unless he is allowed to have this intellectual concept and to carry it out freely, his work is not art, and it is not human. That is, responsibility is essential to human work.

Man is an intellectual, fully responsible being. Anything

which damages his intellectual capacity or reduces or removes his responsibility, is intolerable to Catholic ethics.

"God provides for everything according to the capacity of its nature. It is natural to man to attain to intellectual truths through sensible objects, because all our knowledge originates from sense."—(St. Thomas 1. 1. 9.)

Hence the educative and perfecting nature of human work.

"The work of a carpenter requiring a certain absolute multitude; namely, art in the soul, the movement of the hand, and a hammer."—(St. Thomas 1. 7. 4.)

My present purpose is confined to the establishment of the Catholic principle that real human work, however simple, is *art*. But it must be, however simple, fully responsible and complete in itself. For a full and conclusive discussion the reader is referred to the works of M. Maritain, especially *Art and Scholasticism*, and to those of Mr. Eric Gill, especially *Work and Property*.

Special attention should be given to the working out by both these writers of the highly important principle that art is a justification for private ownership. As Maritain concludes (*Freedom in the Modern World*, p. 197): "The principle holds good whether the work be that of a craftsman or a manual labourer."

There is little point in assembling here the numerous testimonies against mechanisation which are to be found in the works of a surprising variety of writers. We may include one by a distinguished and thoroughly responsible Catholic sociologist:

"From the social point of view, mechanisation seems to have had grave drawbacks. First relatively to society in general, by the excessive vulgarisation of luxury, comfort and cheap superfluity. Secondly, and above all, to the workers, for whom machines have the following grave disadvantages. They lower the intellectual level of the workman, work being, in fact, done automatically and entirely by the machine. The workman in attendance is reduced to a secondary, monotonous, unintelligent role. He is the servant of the machine. He is its accessory. Finally, he becomes a mere cog, an impersonal automaton, and relatively insignificant."—(Belliot: *Manuel de Sociologie Catholique*, p. 225.)

Pius XI, in *Quadragesimo Anno* (p. 53.4), discusses and rejects the principle that since economic production (under socialism) must be carried on collectively, "Men must surrender themselves wholly to society. ... The loss of human dignity which results from these socialised methods of work will be easily compensated for by the abundance of goods." The principle here condemned applies also to any industrialised method, for the same reasons.

"It is evident that in things done by man, the chief act is that of command to which all the rest are subordinate." (1. 11. 57-6.) But as under advanced Industrialism motions are as nearly automatic as possible there is no command and the work is not human.

"Any industrial or manufacturing theory or system or practice which 'reduces men to a subhuman condition of intellectual irresponsibility' (D'Arcy) or tends to do so, is to be condemned. Therefore modern machine-industrialism and mass production is to be condemned, and no degree of responsibility in 'leisure time' is a compensation for irresponsibility in 'working time.' Culture is a product of work."—(Gill, *Work and Property*, p. 3.)

It remains true that a real grasp of the nature of Industrialism is rare. Its victims, normally, have heard of nothing else, and cannot make the necessary mental contrasts. Those who are physically near to, but economically remote from it, suffer from that extraordinary segregation which is one of the most notable features of modern times. Such a person, for example, rarely has occasion to travel by public vehicle during the "rush hours," when he would have an opportunity of seeing for himself the mental and physical exhaustion, or alternatively the febrile excitement, of those who have spent the long day in a machine or assembly shop. Some writers seem to have formed a clear mental picture. Others, not less eminent, show no signs of having done so.

With some reluctance, and only because of its gravity, I must point out a rare case of this kind in M. Maritain's *Freedom in the Modern World*. On pages 61 and 62 of that work he discusses favourably a "frame and constitution of industrial life which would be fundamentally different from that of agriculture." He considers that on a "Guild" basis, it is tolerable that "the servitude that follows use of the machine shall be offset by admitting the workers to share in the direction." I have stated above that such a collective ownership would be preferable in itself to the present wage-system, but the cession is regrettable for other reasons. He goes on to say that agricultural economy should tend to the restoration of family economy and family and peasant ownership. Evidently M. Maritain has not realised the main effect of the "pluralist" principle which he endorses. This has been discussed in the preceding chapter, as being the condition of severe strain set up between the two systems. M. Maritain will need no reminder from me of the effect of such a strain. On an earlier page he has said that it is impossible "to rationalise the production of a factory without knowing what a factory is." (p. 14.)

I hope I may add, without offence to a philosopher to whom my debt is great, that a closer acquaintance with the momentum of industrialised production would have made this suggestion of pluralism impossible to him.

Moreover "Factory" Guild, where the ownership is common, seems here at variance with two of the three justifications of private property quoted from St. Thomas in

Chapter V.

This being so, it seems clear that a collective industrial Guild can have no more than a temporary validity. The permanently valid principle is integral personal ownership, on which alone the Guild can properly be based.

I said at the beginning of the last chapter that Industrialism operated by subdivision and segregation of processes. Perhaps "segregation" is the real key. It is the whole point of a factory, that the production of an article is divided into short stages, whether of manufacture or of assembly. Otherwise there would be no point in a factory at all. For if a workman made a whole article, he might as easily do so, frequently, in a shed in his back garden as in a factory. It is true that in some few cases, developed usually from the more ancient crafts, there is some approximation to completeness of operation. Pottery works sometimes show evidence of this, but it is exceptional. By some obscure law of compensatory damnation, this class of factory usually has the most disgusting layout and surroundings.

On the other hand, the fully developed forms of Industrialism, such as motor cars and chocolates, combine a sort of surgical hygiene with the final degradations in sub-division of work.

The irresponsibility of industrial work has been emphasised, and correctly, since it affects the bulk of its victims, but it would be a mistake to suppose that there is no responsibility in a factory. Biologists describe a particular operation of heredity as a "segregation of unit characters." This is a fairly exact definition of industrial processes. The aim of modern industrialists is to allow to each mechanic one only operation, the simpler the better. We are all familiar with the travelling belt since Mr. Chaplin's *Modern Times*, and the tragedy is that the thing was not a satire by exaggeration, but by understatement. Perhaps we are not so familiar with the automatic lathe and press, where a single operation of supreme simplicity and monotony is all that is required from the tender. And still less are we familiar with the more skilled workman who stands as one of a row, all constrained by the power shafting to a speed dictated by the foreman, whose job it is to speed up the shafting to the limit of endurance.

But there *are* responsible mechanics and designers, also under the harrow of unit segregation. For they suffer by excess of responsibility and not by defect. The designer or draughtsman may easily be the cause of scrapping the whole output of a part or parts, because they have been given tolerances inappropriate to other parts with which, much later, they are to be associated. The toolmaker and fitter also suffer by excess and not by defect.

But these, with the tenders and assemblers, are all in like case. None is responsible for a *complete* piece of work. All suffer acutely by fear of the sack, even more acutely by reason of a speed fiendishly designed to work to the maximum of what the "human factor" will stand.

I think it is fair to add that one feature alone, that of *dictated speed*, is enough to reduce industrial work to that "condition of sub-human irresponsibility" which has been referred to above. And in the nature of the case, power speed must be *dictated* to the individual worker under any conceivable industrial variant.

There is a dreadful story of a girl who went to a Doctor suffering from neurasthenia, and explained that her job was to fit the A key to typewriters on a travelling assembly belt; "Oh, Doctor," she cried, "if they let me do the letter B!"

"Work," says Cardinal Hinsley, "should be the normal means of serving God, not, as it so often is, a positive obstacle to His service." How can the "single-operation slave," or for that matter, the harassed designer or fitter, worship God in his work?

This is not the place to discuss a disturbing point to which I have referred elsewhere. I mean the tendency for the Catholic

Youth Movement to be encouraged in a technique of immolation to Industrialism. The Movement is very dear to the heart of the present Pope. I think it need only be said that ode of its original principles was "To Christianise the environment of work." In the light of the facts and principles here disclosed this can, I submit, have only one tolerable meaning.

Dr. Carrel, in the work already quoted, adds these pertinent words:

"Esthetic activity remains potential in most individuals because industriail civilisation has surrounded them with coarse, vulgar, and ugly sights. Because we have been transformed into machines. The worker spends his life repeating the same gesture thousands of times each day. He manufactures only single parts. He never makes the complete object. He is not allowed to use his intelligence. He is the blind horse plodding round and round the whole day long to draw water from a well. Industrialism forbids man the very mental activities which would bring him every day some joy. In sacrificing mind to matter, modern civilisation has perpetrated a momentous error. An error all the more dangerous because nobody revolts against it, because it is accepted as easily as the unhealthy life of great cities and the confinement in factories."

It is this stinking inferno, from which anyone not bound to it keeps his careful distance, that Catholics, especially young Catholics, are to enter and Christianise. "The possession of an immortal soul," says the Cardinal, "gives all God's creatures and children certain rights."

One of them is to copy the rich in this at least, and to keep out of the modern factory.

So far we have considered Industrialism as a going concern. It remains to make some brief analysis of its efficient cause, the machine.

It threatens to become a Frankenstein to its creator, and

many of the most intelligent people of the world are challenging or doubting its use to man. For it has a mark which was absent from former oppressions. The old tyrannies were the work of human wills. If these could be changed or overcome the oppression ceased. But the machine seems to have a dreadful momentum of its own, independent of the wills of our masters. This may be illusion, due merely to the multiplicity of wills concerned, but I do not think it fanciful to see in the present problem a complication of hypnosis. It is as though, for the first time in history, man is unable to destroy what he has made.

However that may be, we must consider here, and more dispassionately, whether the Catholic ethic has anything to say about machine production as such. Clearly we shall find nothing direct in the Doctors, for machinery in our sense did not exist. And for the same reasons as obtain in the case of Capitalism, a direct condemnation is of its nature impossible. As Capitalism is a disease of property, so Industrialism is a disease of work. We must apply the eternal principles, to state which has been the effort of this book.

It is difficult to define a machine, and some writers have used the fact to darken counsel. Mr. Chesterton, on this subject, used the "fallacy of the accumulating heap" to silence them. There may be difference of opinion on whether a plough is a machine, but none that a reaper and binder is one. Where exactly in between occurs the "dividing line" of which some writers are so fond, is immaterial.

The matter may be discussed briefly under four headings :

1. "Machinery," as K. L. Kenrick says, "makes property indivisible." And since the essence of property lies in its control, this is clearly true. But property is a natural right, and if the machine impedes it, the machine must go and not property.

2. Machinery makes personal skill obsolescent. How many

arts are lost entirely, and others dying, by its introduction? But all human skill is of help to sanctification, and the reduction of the relative operations to a brute machine is therefore damaging to human personality.

3. But Machinery, it is said, enables us to avoid drudgery. It is false. Every art has an element of hard work, which is part of the discipline of the job. If work is complete, the craftsman has the discipline of the "drudgery," and the joy of the craft, in the one task. It is a mark of Industrialism to have segregated drudgery, as when a few poor wretches have to look after the sewage of a whole community. In normal forms of life, every man does this for himself, as part of his self-discipline.

Or when the extremely clean and convenient electric light involves the existence of huge generating stations which deface and foul half a town or half a county, *elsewhere.*

4. There are machines which require skill to use, as motor cars. In these cases wider principles must be invoked. On the one hand that society must be diseased if, in great proportion, the citizens at any given moment are where they do not wish to be. For to remedy this is the only use of cars.

On the other hand, use of a machine must include an investigation into the necessary methods of its manufacture, and if these are inadmissible by the main principles of ethics, the machine should not be used even if it is, in its finished form, innocuous.

I have never seen any force in the argument that to scrap the machine would drive us into poverty and drudgery. It all depends on the organisation of the new society. So far as my historical reading goes, drudgery only existed when the conditions of oppression were present, and there are numerous examples of happy societies in the past. That, however, is not the point. I am convinced that all *industrial* machinery should go, on the strictest Catholic principles, and irrespective of whether we become poor or not, but of course in due deliberation and order. As regards other kinds of machinery, I am content to abide by the principles laid down by the late Arthur Penty.

1. The use of machinery should be restricted where it conflicts with the claims of personality—that is, it should not be allowed to turn men into robots.
2. It should not be allowed where it is injurious to health.
3. It should not be allowed to create economic disorder like unemployment.
4. It should not be allowed where it conflicts with the claims of the crafts and arts.
5. It should not be allowed to multiply commodities beyond the point at which natural demand is satisfied—that is, beyond the point at which sales need to be artificially stimulated by advertisement.
6. It should not be allowed to trespass seriously upon the world's supply of irreplaceable raw material.

My readers may care to reflect on how much mechanisation would be left if every one of these irrefutable conditions were applied.

We should remember in conclusion that as St. Thomas points out, "A false reason can corrupt the habit of a true opinion, or even of science."—(2. 1. 53. 1.) It is no answer to these points to urge the innocence of machinery as such. The real test is why it is used and what is its effect.

XI: FINANCE AND COMMERCE

Better is a little with Justice, than great revenues with Iniquity.
—Proverbs xvi, 8.

No Christian should be a merchant, because a merchant can rarely or never please God.—Attributed to St. John Chrysostom by St. Antoninus of Florence: Summa Moralis.

It is characteristic and significant that the Fathers and the Schoolmen approach this subject with great suspicion. As this is not an historical survey, it is unnecessary to discuss the incidence of this suspicion. The Catholic philosophy is stated with startling finality by St. Thomas. I say startling, because the infraction of the principle he invokes is a complete explanation of the modern world. It is precisely that all human operations, and even the tokens of operations, should be anchored to the sanity of natural things. In other words it is an application of the principle that Grace does not supersede nature, but presupposes and builds on it.

The subject is vital enough to justify lengthy quotation.

As with another vital principle discussed in an earlier chapter St. Thomas returns more than once to its statement. We find it in brief form in I. II. 2. 1. ad 3. "The desire for natural riches is not infinite, because they suffice for nature in a certain measure. *But the desire for artificial wealth is infinite,* for it is the servant of disordered concupiscence."—(Italics mine.)

He returns to the principle in II. II. 77. 4:

"A tradesman is one whose business consists in the exchange of things. According to the Philosopher (Polit. 1), exchange of things is twofold; one, natural as it were, and necessary, whereby one commodity is exchanged for another, or money taken in exchange for a commodity, in order to satisfy the needs of life. Such like trading, properly speaking, does not belong to tradesmen, but rather to housekeepers or civil servants who have to provide the household or the state with the necessaries of life. The other kind of exchange is either that of money for money, or of any commodity for money, not on account of the necessities of life, but for profit, and this kind of exchange, properly speaking, regards tradesmen according to the Philosopher (Polit. 1.) The former kind of exchange is commendable because it supplies a natural need: *but the latter is deserving of blame, because, considered in itself, it satisfies the greed for gain, which knows no limit and tends to infinity.* Hence trading, considered in itself, has a certain debasement attaching thereto, in so far as, by its very nature, it does not imply a virtuous or necessary end. Nevertheless gain which is the end of trading, though not implying, by its nature, anything virtuous or necessary, does not, in itself, connote anything sinful or contrary to virtue: wherefore nothing prevents gain from being directed to some necessary or even virtuous end, and thus trading becomes lawful. Thus, for instance, a man may intend the moderate gain which he seeks to acquire by trading for the upkeep of his household, or for the assistance of the needy: or again, a man may take to trade for some public advantage, for instance, lest his country lack the necessaries of life, and seek gain, not as an end, but as payment for his labour."—(Italics mine.)

It is clear at once in what consists the danger of finance and commerce. It is that process which does not seek to supply a human need, but seeks profit as a primary object. This is against good morals for two reasons, that greed of gain as such is a sin because it is a perversion of right order, and that operations arising from it are without the safeguard given by an anchor to reality. As I have said, it is a clear description, almost a prophecy, of what is wrong with the modern world. It explains the enormous bucketing momentum of Industrialism, since industrial production is not to satisfy known and existing needs, but so to flood the market that much profit may be made. Hence the recurrent booms and slumps. A man may be greedy. He may desire five horses, or five hundred horses. He will not desire five million horses, since they would be beyond the possibility of use or selection. But he may, and usually will, desire five million pounds, and then another five million, *and so to infinity.*

Quite clearly, the principle includes manufacture for a known market, and excludes manufacture for an unknown one. We have again the principle of directness as against indirectness. So luminous is this reference to the tendency to infinity of tokens divorced from reality, that further discussion would be to darken counsel. I leave it in all its brilliance to the modernists.

Apart from any question of personal dishonesty in the narrow sense, much of the modern distress arises from the fact that finance and credit are a gigantic confidence trick.

The origin of the Bank was that of a safe deposit. In simpler and happier times currency, which was based always on metals of an intrinsic value, was fixed in amount, and held either in circulation, in private hoards, or in safe deposits. Once the growing complications of Industrialism favoured general deposit banking, it was an obvious reflection to the Bankers that not all their depositors would need their money at the same time. Hence the transactions began to exceed the total of the currency deposited. Bankers began to feel their way upwards to a limit of *creation of credit.* Until this process reached the proportions of a pseudo-science, Bankers were always making optimistic mistakes about this limit. Hence the "Runs on the Bank" which were so frequent in early industrial times. The Bankers, with the powerful help of High Finance, have now learned better. They are no longer bankrupted because they create credit whenever they are short of it.

The proportion of credit to currency is astonishing. It may be eight, ten, or twelve to one. The latter figure has rarely been exceeded without disaster. Hence the confidence trick. And hence the grotesque assessments of modern wealth as compared with the standards of the past. Since deposit and finance-wealth is relatively unreal, a feverish economic activity is necessary to maintain the illusion and to pay interest on the all-pervading loans.

It would be improper to do more than refer to this fact in such a work as the present. Nor do I wish to criticise here those remedies which depend entirely on credit reforms of various kinds. No one can be unsympathetic in view of their obvious good-will. They seem to me unsound because: whatever is wrong with the modern world, it is not *merely* a matter of bookkeeping. It is of high importance all the same. I cannot justify in this place a more definite statement than that, other things being equal, Catholic philosophy would prefer currency to be of intrinsic value, by deduction from the main principle of anchoring operations to reality.

The Church has always condemned Usury, and still condemns it. Usury is interest on a loan.[5] It is condemned repeatedly in the Old and New Testaments and by all subsequent authorities. It is still prevalent, as we know from Leo XIII: "The mischief has been increased by rapacious usury, which though more than once condemned by the Church, is … still practised by covetous and grasping men."—(*Rerum Novarum.*)

St. Thomas gives a characteristically final reason for the condemnation:

---

[5] It is widely agreed that this applies strictly, whether the loan be "productive" or "unproductive." Besides the Schoolmen, such modern writers as De la Tour du Pin, Ryan, Belliot, and Maritain endorse this view.

"To take usury for money lent is unjust in itself, because this is to sell what does not exist, and this evidently leads to inequality, which is contrary to justice.

"In order to make this evident, we must observe that there are certain things the use of which consists in their consumption: thus we consume wine when we use it for drink, and we consume wheat when we use it for food. Wherefore in suchlike things the use of the thing must not be reckoned apart from the thing itself, and whoever is granted the use of the thing, is granted the thing itself; and for this reason, to lend things of this kind is to transfer the ownership. Accordingly if a man wanted to sell wine separately from the use of the wine, he would be selling the same thing twice, or he would be selling what does not exist, wherefore he would evidently commit a sin of injustice. In like manner he commits an injustice who lends wine or wheat, and asks for double payment, viz. one, the return of the thing in equal measure, the other, the price of the use, which is called usury."—(2. 2. 78. 1.)

St. Thomas allows interest to be taken for certain *extrinsic* reasons. These are well known and need not detain us, for the modern complications have made it necessary to invoke another principle when discussing modern forms of investment.

Money is naturally sterile.

But so numerous, as compared with the past, are the opportunities of profitable investment, that economists, including some Catholics, have advanced the theory that money is now naturally or equivalently productive. The contention is against common sense, for a piece of metal or paper can be no more fecund now than it was in the Middle Ages. Belliot, for instance, confirms that "all capital is of itself sterile, economically speaking (and not only money) … All capital is unproductive of itself until human labour makes it fructify."—(*Op. cit.* p. 141.)

But in view of these complications, the invocation of the

extrinsic titles has become, not indeed more valid, but certainly more plausible, and for the sake of finality it seems better to attempt a more radical test of investment in its modern form. In my judgment, it is this characteristic *confusion by complication* of modern economics which is responsible for the apparent abrogation of the strict Catholic teaching against usury. It has not been abrogated. In the smoke screen of finance and accounting it cannot be applied and insisted on by the Confessor and Philosopher. Let us see if we can get behind the screen.

For the reasons given, there can be no finality about a discussion of usury alone when proposed about the modern complications. Nor, for that matter, can there be finality in justice about any discussion on money alone. For it remains true that money is only a token and realities must be resolved by realities.

The essence of a usurious loan is that property in the loan passes from the lender to the borrower, as in simple money-lending. The question thus becomes bound up at once with the central Catholic teaching on property. So far as I am aware, the most recent decisions of the Church on the taking of interest are contained in the Encyclical *Vix Pervenit* of Pope Benedict XIV, and the recently revised codex of Canon Law.

It is laid down that where other conditions are fulfilled, interest on a loan may be justified *if property in the loan be retained*. The essence of property, as laid down by Leo XIII in *Rerum Novarum*, consists in its disposal, or as we should say more colloquially, in its control. Now if *Property* be retained, *Responsibility* is retained, since irresponsible property is, for Catholics at least, excluded by the whole body of Moral Theology.

If these considerations are valid, and I see no escape from them, it must be concluded that practically the whole of modern industrial and financial investment is not tolerable to Catholic morals. I have no extreme cases in mind. I mean the normal and almost universal form of investment in a Limited Liability Company, Corporation Stock, and State Loans.

The investor, unless he be a very rich man to begin with, cannot normally secure a controlling share in any enterprise. That function is reserved to professional promoters and financiers, who confine their holdings systematically to 51 per cent. and obtain the other 49 per cent. from the investing public, including investing Catholics.[6]

Let us see how it works out.

A. Mr. Blank sees a prospectus for a new periodical, total capital £100,000. He invests £1,000. After a time the controllers of the enterprise change their policy and advocate, say, contraception or nudism or what not. Mr. Blank is helpless. He cannot even demand his money back, since his only way of withdrawing is to sell his shares on the open market if he can find a buyer, *and the evil started his money goes on.*

B. Mr. Blank then puts his £1,000 into an Investment Trust. He thus loses even the choice of investment, and the Trust may be helping a dozen dubious or immoral enterprises without his knowledge, since it is a physical impossibility for him to keep watch on the operations of all the concerns in which the Trust holds shares.

C. Mr. Blank sells these shares and puts the money into a new Cinema being built by a syndicate in the next street. After a time the Church authorities tell him that the Cinema stinks of the pit.

D. So Mr. Blank puts his money into the nearest Bank, and

---

[6] Fifty-one per cent. must be understood to be a conventional figure. In many cases, the articles of a limited liability company provide for control by a small fraction of the invested capital—held, naturally, by the financiers concerned.

then he is lost indeed, for the Bank is certainly advancing his money to Cinema, Investment Trust; and Pornographic Newspaper alike.

E. In despair, he puts his money into Babylon 2 3/4 per cent. Corporation Loan, and Babylon uses it to start Contraception Clinics.

Throughout this range, there is, in addition to the points mentioned, the whole social duty which need not be detailed here, and especially a definite responsibility on Mr. Blank to see that all these concerns pay a just wage and refrain from grinding the faces of their employees. How is Mr. Blank to know or prove it? And by definition, ignorance is not enough.

These are not cases of far-fetched investment. They are normal cases.

Under the conditions of the older Europe, where an investor was necessarily a partner, he could *stop* anything of which he disapproved by demanding his money. That is, he exercised control and responsibility. That, it seems, is a necessary condition for the investor, and where it is absent the permission of the Church to take interest does not, or should not, apply.

Almost the only modern investments where both elements are present are Land and House Property, and Partnerships in small businesses.

I advance this thesis for the fourth time in public over a period of some thirteen years. On each occasion I have asked to be answered, but no answer has been forthcoming. Perhaps it may be taken, without presumption that if there is no answer forthcoming now, it is because there is no answer.

"Happiness, we say, is the ultimate end of our desires. Now the movement of desire does not go on to infinity, else natural desire would be vain since infinity cannot be traversed. … Whence happiness is called the perfect good, inasmuch as it comprises in itself all things desired."—(St. Thomas, *De Regimine Principum.*)

XII: SELF-SUFFICIENCY AND THE LAND

And the rain fell, and the floods came, and the wind blew, and they beat upon that house, and it fell not, for it was founded upon a rock.
—Matt. vii, 25.

So is the Kingdom God, as if a man should cast seed into the earth ... for the earth of itsehlf bringeth forth fruit, first the blade, then the ear. Afterwards the full corn in the ear.—Mark iv, 26-28.

It is recorded by St. Justin Martyr, who lived in sub-apostolic times, that St. Joseph was a maker of agricultural implements.

I have tried to exclude sentiment and sentimentality from this discussion, even if not my anger. If the Popes, the most responsible authorities in the world, can be unrestrained in their denunciation of its wickedness and injustice, I see no need for a false detached calmness in the laity. "Shall not the teeth of the children be set on edge?"

But everything our Lord did was significant and a lesson for us, and I cannot think it exceptionally purposeless that He was a craftsman in immediate contact with the life of the land. Nearly all His figures are of gracious nature. He Who knew all the kingdoms of the world, and the glory of them, Who might have fired His hearers with tales of high adventure such as they loved, chose instead to speak of sheep and their owner, of threshing floors and barns, and the lilies of the field.

Père F. M. Braun, O.P., has expressed this thought more practically in a recent essay (La Vie Spirituelle, translated in *Blackfriars*, Jan. 1938):

"The humble condition which this manual labour indicates is in no way comparable to that of our modern proletariat. ... The occupation which Jesus pursued was not one of those which by burdening the body with fatigue or monotony prevents the free play of the mind. … The manual labour to which Jesus devoted Himself was therefore *Human*. The type of worker whom we revere in the artisan of Nazareth is that which corresponds most closely to our ideal of life, to which mediæval conditions sought to approximate, and to which recent Papal Encyclicals have sought to guide the manual labourer of to-day."

For my part, I will not allow to any Catholic the licence to be supercilious when it is a question of the kind of life chosen by the Sun of Justice.

Penty, in his *Guildsman's Interpretation of History*, quotes the following passages from the great work of Janssen, *The German People at the Close of the Middle Ages*:

"Among manual industries none stood higher in the estimation of the Canon Law than agriculture. It was looked upon as the mother and producer of all social organisation and all culture, as the fosterer of all other industries, and consequently as the basis of national well-being. The Canon Law exacted special consideration for agriculture, and partly for this reason, that it tended in a higher degree than any other branch of labour to teach these who practised it godly fear and uprightness. 'The farmer,' so it is written in *A Christian Admonition*, 'must in all things be protected and encouraged, for all depend on his labour, from the Emperor to the humblest of mankind, and his handiwork is in particular honourable and well-pleasing to God;' therefore both the spiritual and the secular law protect him."

"Next to agriculture came handiwork. 'This is praiseworthy in the sight of God, especially in so far as it represents necessary and useful things.' And when the articles are made with care and art, then both God and men take pleasure in them; and it is good and true work when artistic men, by the skill and cunning of their hands, in beautiful building and sculpture, spread the glory of

God and make men gentle in their spirits, so that they find delight in beautiful things, and look reverently on all art and handicraft as a gift of God for the use, enjoyment, and edification of mankind."

This, I submit, is of permanent, and not merely of temporary Catholic value.

The Father of Monasticism, whose wise Rule has endured for thirteen hundred years, says: "Then are they truly Monks, when they live by the labour of their hands, as did our fathers and the Apostles."—(Rule of St. Benedict.)

I suggest that this life, so revered by Our Lord and the Fathers, and so contemned by our dying world, is a fitting example for us who have to build anew from the ruins and dust in which we are doomed to live.

Life on the Land, as we saw in an earlier chapter, corresponds uniquely to the Catholic concepts of a sound social basis. It has the further advantage that its essential structure still remains. Pius XI, in *Quadragesimo Anno*, has this highly significant passage:

"It is true that even to-day these economic conditions do not everywhere exist exclusively, for there is another economic system which still embraces a very large and influential group of men. There are, for instance, the agricultural classes, who form the larger portion of the human family, and who find in their occupation the means of obtaining honestly and justly what is needful for their maintenance. This system too has its difficulties and problems, of which Our Predecessor spoke repeatedly. ... But it is the capitalist economic regime that ... has invaded and pervaded ... intimately affecting them by its advantages, inconveniences and vices."

The lesson has been driven home by many other authorities. A recent joint statement by the Mid-Western Bishops of the United States may be quoted in support:

"The first duty of the farmer is not to produce, but to live; and to live in a manner befitting his worth as a man and his dignity as a child of God. There should be in the occupation of the farmer a dignity and independence that are not possible in the collective mass-production enterprises of modern industry. …

"The radical evil of the economic situation, which has now become world-wide, is that everything is judged from the standpoint of the market. This has condemned the farm to world competition in its system of production. Under such conditions the farmer's living is subject to hazards over which he has no control; and he is, by the system of which he forms part, exposed to the vicissitudes and temptations of blind speculation. His production is fed into the currents of international trade; and he is deprived of the opportunity of dealing with the local and neighbourhood interests. The production of the farm has to a dominant extent followed and adopted the purpose and the system of industry in which all goods are produced, not for use, but for sale. It is to the public interest that the area of production for use, or for neighbourhood and local exchange, be fostered and enlarged. It is desirable that changes be effected that will enable the American farmer to feel that all his interests are not bound up in the market. …"

"We heartily commend the principle advocated for the American farmer by some important agricultural associations, namely, the small holdings and individual ownership. We look on the farm as an important economic means of sustaining the normal family life and of supplying the nation with a healthy population and a self-respecting and independent citizenry that will give us a sound leadership. … We are opposed to the industrialisation of American agriculture and to the system of corporate farming. The farm is primarily a place to live and to make a living."

It seems clear therefore, that with much evidence, summarised briefly in earlier chapters, that Industrialism holds out no promise of permanence, but rather of decline and of sterility, a return to the Land is at once the most direct and the most strategic Catholic reaction.

To quote again my friend K. L. Kenrick :

"By following these trains of thought we are enabled to arrive at our final charge against the modern world, which is that it divides society into two classes—a smaller possessed of rights with no appreciable duties, and a much larger possessed of duties with no appreciable rights. This is the fundamental injustice of the industrial system. No analysis which tries to conceal this essential feature of the system can lead us anywhere. Clearly the most important duties are those performed by the men who work on the land to produce food for the whole community. Practically the most valued rights are the 'sacred rights of property.' The sponsors of the Land Movement claim that the first act of Catholic Social Justice should be to confer the most valued rights upon those who perform the most important duties. They further maintain that to suggest any less reform as characteristically Catholic is to disregard the express wishes of Cardinals and Popes."—(*The Cross and the Plough, Ladyday,* 1938.)

Moreover, I must repeat here briefly a consideration already touched upon. It is not seriously disputed that industrialised populations are tending rapidly to extinction. But in England and America, the Catholic populations are some four times more urbanised than even the general population. Our birth-rates, it is clear from many statistical enquiries, are not noticeably better than those of the surrounding populations. A return to the Land is not really of choice in any industrialised country. For the Catholic bodies of England and America it is both imperative and urgent.

In my judgment, therefore, the main line of Catholic Action

should be to set up on the Land self-sufficient Catholic communities for a triple purpose. (1) To enable Catholics to practise the cardinal virtues in an integral life (as is plainly impossible, short of heroic virtue, in our cities). (2) To utilise the good life so achieved in order to prevent the impending sterility of the urbanised Catholic bodies in England and America, and (3) to react in due time on what is left of the cities, and so play a due part in the salvation of the world.

For this, a large measure of self-sufficiency will be not only desirable but necessary. In some Catholic quarters, self-sufficiency is contemned. Evidently the plain reason given by St. Thomas, that a thing is the more perfect the more it is self-sufficient, does not convince them. Perhaps they will be convinced by an apostle of modernism, seeing, perhaps too late, the end of our universal taking in of one another's washing. Mr. J.M. Keynes, writing in the *New Statesman* in August 1933, has this passage:

"I sympathise, therefore, with those who would minimise, rather than those who would maximise, economic entanglement between nations. Ideas, knowledge, art, hospitality, travel—these are the things which should of their nature be international. But let goods be homespun whenever it is reasonably and conveniently possible. ... The decadent international but individualistic capitalism, in the hands of which we found ourselves after the war, is not a success. It is not intelligent, it is not beautiful, it is not virtuous. ... and it doesn't deliver the goods. In short, we dislike it, and we are beginning to despise it."

The technique of such a return to simplicity and sanity on the land has not been worked out completely, because it has not yet been put properly into practice. Many mistakes have been made and will be made. But enough is known and proved to ensure its ultimate success. I suggest as the essential framework of such a return, the following factors :

1. It must be on a scale, after a brief period of experiment, as large as possible.
2. If the State will not finance it, it must be financed by "the willing sacrifice of Catholic wealth."
3. It must consist of fully-rounded communities, containing besides the farmers themselves all essential services: craftsmen, priest, doctor and/or nurse, schools. Individual communities must be large enough almost from the start to permit of such rounding.
4. These communities must be self-subsistent to the fullest possible extent. That is, they must provide for almost all their own needs, and trade with the outside world only for exceptional goods, taxation, and so on.
5. They must be based firmly and irrevocably upon widely distributed productive property.
6. They must be banded, on this basis, in Guilds, which can have surprisingly wide powers if the safeguard of private ownership be present.
7. They must have fully competent technical direction for an adequate period, but this direction must understand and approve the Catholic philosophy of the Return.

This end will not be achieved by following the lines of many of the doctrinaires in this field, and making the countrysides as much like the towns as possible.

It seems clear that it is the immaterial content of our urban environment, quite as much as the material content, which is tending to sterility and decline.

I am aware that until we regain the tone of our fathers, many concessions have to be made to our softness. This will not be a danger if the end in view is kept clearly in mind by all concerned.

I am not in favour of any form of mechanisation in agriculture, for the severely practical reason that machinery on the land serves only one purpose. It enables fewer men to cultivate a given acreage, or (what is the same thing) it enables an equal number of men to cultivate a larger acreage. It is thus, *of its nature*, hostile to communities of small men, for it provides an irresistible temptation to increase acreage and thus to destroy intimacy and balance. The older technique of farming provides adequately against all reasonable difficulties due to weather conditions.

Finally, I will not accept the position that the task is impossible. To repeat a principle I have used many times, it is incumbent upon anyone who believes in God to hold that if a thing ought to be done, it can be done.

And since, by the severest logic, our survival depends upon a return to the Land, this is supremely a thing that ought to be done.

XIII: CONCLUSIONS

Whose fan is in His hand, and He will purge His floor, and will gather the wheat into His barn.—Luke 3, 17.

I have compassion on the multitude.—Mark viii, 2.
Man goeth forth to his work, and to his labour, until the evening.
—Psalm 103.

Within the limits possible to a work of this modest size, we have now been able to see that *Vision of the Structure*—that part of the eternal reason of God which concerns Social Justice—set out as our aim in the first chapter.

We have seen that man is not a "hand," to be given so much of bread and circuses as will keep him alive and quiet, but a Person, with attributes and rights drawn from his likeness to God.

We have seen that the Family, the primal human society, is not something created or tolerated by the State, but on the contrary is its unit and its archetype.

We have seen that organic bodies, and the State itself, are for man, and not man for them.

We have seen that man, as a fully responsible Person, needs, and may demand as a right, independent control of sufficient assets for his needs. That is, the institution of Private Property is necessary to man, and necessary to *every* man for his full development.

We have seen that by the severest deduction from necessary principles, a certain form of society is preferred and envisaged by the Church.

We have seen that any temporary tolerances in Catholic teaching are solely for the purpose of facilitating a change to the permanent basis of Justice, in due time and order.

We have seen that besides the successive components of Justice, they must occur in due order for their due effect. Thus Guilds are not a substitute for Property, but a buttress for Property having prior existence.

We have considered one by one the functions of Modern Industrialism, and have seen that in some respects they are temporarily tolerable, and in others intolerable, but that none of them is in full accord with the permanent Catholic Teaching.

And since it is the purpose of thought, and especially of Catholic thought, to issue in necessary action, we have now to consider how this structure, from being a fortifying vision, may be made a concrete reality on the earth where God has placed us.

In order to indicate the necessary lines of such action, we must distinguish between what action is imperative, and therefore the duty of all, and what action is to be ruled by prudence, expediency and perhaps a personal selectivity by way of vocation to Social Justice.

I think there are three features of the Modern World against which Catholic reaction must be universal and of obligation, regardless of consequences even to public order.

1. We must oppose the modern tendency to reestablish slavery. "Servitude," says St. Thomas, "is a hindrance to the good use of power" (11. 1. 2. 4 ad 3). Freedom is the necessary basis of Catholicism. After having led Europe from a slave basis to a free, we can tolerate no return.

2. The God of the Church is the same as the God of Biology, Whose laws may not be broken with impunity. We can tolerate, therefore, no social basis which is tending to human sterility and extinction. Therefore our reaction must be radical and persistent, conditioned only by the primary duty of living at all.

3. Personality is the prime human attribute. Therefore we

can participate in no system which damages or destroys it.

Here again, the only condition is the necessity to live.

The duty of reaction under all these heads will fall chiefly on those who are not personally under the harrow of Industrialism. This emancipated class, up to the present, has been far too complacent towards a system of which it is the sole beneficiary. It must cease to draw its benefits from two of the four sins crying to Heaven for vengeance, and it must add the weight of its freedom to achieve the freedom of the sons of God. It is vital that in the meantime the poor and dispossessed be kept in possession of one thing at least—the eternal standards.

I do not think that the task, during the next generation, will be as difficult as it has seemed hitherto. It is quite clear that apart from a few worshippers of the machine like Mr. Wells, an increasing multitude of intelligent men and women all over the world, and of all shades of religious and political opinion, are convinced that civilisation is headed for disaster. Only the brutal inertia of finance and industrialism prevents early action. And in the long run, ideas must prevail over a system whose only dynamic is greed of gain. Several short-sighted writers have advanced the opinion that so dominant and pervading an organism as Capitalist Industrialism must be fought in the same way as the Old Slave State. That is, by ceding to force, accepting the conditions, however destructive of right reason, and working over many generations for their gradual supersession.

It would in any case be disgraceful in us to do this, for whereas the Church was born into a Slave State, she saw the birth of Industrialism, and by anticipation and by Papal reaction she advanced principles that should have killed it in its youth had we responded to the lead. If we have to go into the Catacombs again, it will be the supreme betrayal of our history.

But there are other grounds for hope. Self-preservation is the strongest instinct in mankind, and as the vices and brutal negations of all forms of Industrialism are seen to threaten the very life of the social body, it seems highly probable that society will turn to any system which escape and life. The Catholic Social system is so clearly the only radical alternative that not hostility, but sympathy and support, may well be ours before many more years have passed.

But for that to happen, non-Catholics also must be able to see *The Vision of the Structure*. On that ground alone, no future social discussion can afford to omit or obscure the permanent and luminous *reason* in Catholic teaching.

For that again, deeds as well as words will be necessary, and it is essential that, whether society be hostile or friendly, practical remedial work upon an ample scale be undertaken by the Catholic body. Some suggestions for the most radical of this work were made in the previous chapter. Others could be added. The essential fact must be that it is our personal business and not merely that of the State.

Action against a hostile position must be by frontal attack or by an outflanking movement. Where it is possible, the latter is always preferable, for where an enemy is entrenched, there he is strongest, and the greater sacrifice is necessary to dislodge him. Therefore, Catholic reaction must, in my judgment, have an *outflanking* character. It does not appear that Finance-Industrialism will ever yield to frontal attacks. On its own chosen ground it is impregnable. For this reason, it seems that attacks based on currency reform alone, or on a continuance of industrialism without the Industrialist, must always fail. There is no point in attacking an enemy where he is strongest and best equipped. In spite of their direct opposition in philosophy, expedients based on Catholic ethics have always this outflanking quality, rather than the other, because error is a defect and the remedy is the whole.

Perhaps I may be allowed to make a further point not

touched on elsewhere. There is much misunderstanding of the Catholic devotion to Poverty. Poverty is necessary to any Catholic system. Our Lord praised it repeatedly, the greatest saints have praised it most.

But Poverty is not destitution. And the modern world, which has lost all the golden means, has no other concept of Poverty than this.

Poverty is life with a "sufficiency of things" and no superfluities. Destitution is its industrial disease, as machine labour is the industrial disease of human work. We need not, then, fear poverty. Poverty in the Catholic Social system means a fuller and happier life than any to be found in our modern world, where "segregation of unit characters" has removed from all classes some part of the human inheritance.

But, if, unhappily, the greater fight be upon us: if we must look forward to a triumphant development of everything we hate, then we must still engage. This is not a battle to be declined, because to decline battle is to be absorbed in the invader, who is Death.

As it has been stated by a great writer quoted frequently in these pages:

"Is Communism compatible with Catholicism? The question is an improper one. The question is: Is Catholicism compatible with the industrial development of Society? The answer is certainly: No. For at the toot of Catholicism is the doctrine of human responsibility, and that State in which human responsibility is denied or diminished is a State in which Catholicism cannot flourish: Man is man all the time, and not only in his spare time. In an industrial State, men, working men, the majority, are only fully responsible when they are not working. In such a State Catholicism returns to the catacombs. Thence she will emerge when the orgasm of industrial triumph has spent itself."

On that note I end. If we must choose, let us prefer to that loss of identity which is Death, the Blanket of the Dark. *"Under which King, Bezonian? Speak or die."*

BIBLIOGRAPHY

(*Confined to works which are either indispensable or readily accessible*)
[Editor's Note: Many of these publications are of course now out of print and very hard to obtain in 2014]

Aquinas, St. Thomas. *Summa Theologica*. English translation. Burns Oates & Washbourne.

Summa Contra Gentiles. English translation. Burns Oates & Washbourne.

On the Governance of Princes. Translated by Rev. Gerald B. Phelan, D.D. Toronto.

Encyclicals, Papal. Chiefly Leo XIII and Pius XI. Catholic Truth Society.

Belliot, R. P. Albéric. *Manuel de Sociologie Catholique*. Lethielleux.

Belloc, Hillaire. *The Servile State*. T.N. Foulis.

Europe and the Faith. Constable.

The Reconstruction of Property. Distributist League.

Carrel, Dr. Alexis. *Man the Unknown*. Hamilton.

Chesterton, G.K. *The Outline of Sanity*. Methuen.

A Short History of England. Chatto & Windus.

Cobbett, William. *Cottage Economy*. Pepler.

Rural Rides. Dent.

Devas, Charles Stanton. *The Key to the World's Progress*. Longmans.

Fream's *Elements of Agriculture*. Murray. (For the present purpose the older editions are preferable.)

Flee to the Fields. The Faith and Works of the Catholic Land Movement. Heath Cranton.

Gill, Eric. *Money and Morals*. Faber & Faber.

The Necessity of Belief. Faber & Faber.

Work and Property. Dent.

Hammond, J.L. and B. *The Town, Village, and Skilled Labourer*. (3 vols.) Longmans.

Hughes, Rev. Philip. *Pope Pius XI*. Sheed & Ward.

Huxley, Aldous. *Brave New World*. Chatto & Windus.

I'll Take My Stand. (The Southern Agrarian Tradition.) By Twelve Southerners. Harper.

Lombroso, Gina. *La Rançon du Machinisme*. Payot.

Lymington, Viscount. *Famine in England*. Witherby.

Maritain, Jacques. *Three Reformers*. Sheed & Ward.
    Art and Scholasticism. Sheed & Ward.
    Religion and Culture. Sheed & Ward.
    Introduction to Philosophy. Sheed & Ward.
    Freedom in the Modern World. Sheed & Ward.

McNabb, Fr. Vincent, O.P., S.T.M. *The Catholic Church and Philosophy*. Burns Oates & Washbourne.
    The Church and the Land. Burns Oates & Washbourne.
    Nazareth or Social Chaos. Burns Oates & Washbourne.

O'Brien, G. *An Essay on Mediæval Economic Teaching*. Longmans.

Penty, Arthur J. *A Guildsman's Interpretation of History*. Allen & Unwin.
    Old Worlds for New. Allen & Unwin.
    Means and Ends. Faber & Faber.

Robbins, H. *An Examination of Eugenics*. Burns Oates & Washbourne.

Rogers, Thorold. *Six Centuries of Work and Wages*. Fisher Unwin.

Shove, Commander Herbert, D.S.O., R.N. *The Fairy Ring of Commerce*. (Out of print.)

Sinclair, Robert. *Metropolitan Man*. Allen & Unwin.

Sombart, Werner. *A New Social Philosophy*. Princetown U.P.

Witcutt, Rev. W. P., LL.B. *The Dying Lands*. Distributist League.

ABOUT THE AUTHOR

[Editors's Note: The following biographical information on Robbins has been kindly provided by IHS Press. The publisher is incredibly grateful to that company for its kind permission to include the text here.]

A Distributist, Catholic land movement activist, journalist, and editor, Harold Robbins (1888-1954) was born in Birmingham to a Protestant family, and converted to Catholicism in the early 1900s, after briefly declaring himself a socialist, as many non-Catholic social thinkers did who were attempting to find a way to distance themselves from the prevailing Manchester liberalism. His conversion is most likely due to, among other things, his having discovered the two most prominent English Catholic writers of his time – Belloc and Chesterton – and their appealing critique of both socialism, about which he was having doubts, and capitalism.

Robbins jumped into the Distributist movement early, attempting unsuccessfully to write for the two weeklies then espousing it, the Eye Witness and its successor the New Witness. After military service in the first world war he became involved in the "New Witness League," founded in 1918 around the weekly for opposing corruption in politics. Robbins was made Chairman of the Birmingham branch, the most active branch of the league. The group's work focused ideologically on Distributism and the opposition to the eugenicist policies then being pursued by the British Ministry of Health. Some of Robbins's thinking on this topic is found in his An Examination of Eugenics (London: Burns, Oates and Washbourne, Ltd., 1930). In the spring of 1921 the league wound up its activities, and two years later the paper of the same name ceased publication.

In 1925 those collaborating on the New Witness gathered around a new paper, G.K.'s Weekly (to which Robbins contributed), begun in order to "promote and ensure the discussion of the real economic forces of the age under their real names," as Chesterton put it. Partly as a natural outgrowth and partly due to its financial straits (which it was in until the demise of its founder in 1936), and the need for subscribers, a league was also formed around this weekly, "for the restoration of liberty by the distribution of property"; or, the Distributist League. Robbins led, as Chairman, the Birmingham Branch of the league from 1926 to 1933, the most active and aggressive branch among some two dozen extant around 1927. He was chiefly instrumental in founding, with Msgr. James Dey, Rector of Oscott College and later Ordinary to the British Armed Forces, the Midlands Catholic Land Association; Robbins was its Honorary Secretary during the years that it was active, 1931 to 1936. This effort translated into practice what Robbins felt was somewhat of an overemphasis on mere talk: it was, he said, a "working model of practical distributism." He also edited the journal of the Catholic Land Associations of England and Wales, The Cross and the Plough, from 1934 to 1946, published by the Catholic Land Federation of England and Wales.

He co-authored with K. L. Kenrick in 1928 what came to be known as "the Birmingham Scheme," a pamphlet entitled Unemployment: A Distributist Solution; his friendship with Kenrick, who was the other chief mover of the Birmingham branch of the league, spanned many years. Kenrick called Robbins the "real power house" of the movement in their area. In 1946 he wrote a short biography of GKC – and also a history of Distributist activism from 1920 to 1940 – dedicated to Kenrick and entitled The Last of the Realists, though it was not published until 1948, and then only serialized in The Cross and the Plough because of wartime restrictions on paper.

Robbins's short but powerful magnum opus was published in 1938 as The Sun of Justice: An Essay on the Social Teaching of the Catholic Church; he expressed its thesis thus: "Social Justice is crucial to the future of the Faith. There are many ways to the Faith, but it is certain that the concept of Our Lord as the Sun of Justice is not only valid, but is the only way by which our disillusioned and despairing world will return to Him" (pp. 10–11). Dorothy Day (1897–1980) noted in a 1954 issue of her paper, The Catholic Worker, that Robbins's Sun of Justice "contains the best thinking ever done on Distributism."